The Greek-o-File
Volume 6

written & edited by

Sylvia & Terry Cook

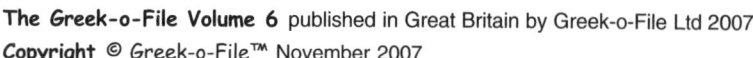

The Greek-o-File Volume 6 published in Great Britain by Greek-o-File Ltd 2007

Copyright © Greek-o-File™ November 2007

ISBN 978-0-9543593-5-5

The Greek-o-File Volume 6 is the latest compendium of new articles and anecdotes in paperback format compiled by Sylvia Cook from the work of many writers including Sylvia & Terry Cook and the contributors acknowledged with their work. Photographs and illustrations were supplied by authors of the articles except where specified, other illustrations are from free to use 'clipart'.

Edited and set: Sylvia Cook

Acknowledgements

As with all our books, it is the enthusiasm, feedback and contributions from subscribers to previous publications that ensure we can continue publishing The Greek-o-Files. We depend on and thank those who continue to support us as direct subscribers, contributors and advertisers and those who tell others about us too.

Our thanks especially to the contributors to this volume and the advertisers, especially those who have supported us for many years, encouraging us as promoters of the 'real Greece' they believe in, as much as for commercial reasons. We and they would be pleased if you would check out their offerings and support them too.

We are indebted to Road Editions for their kind permission to reproduce, adapt and use their maps to illustrate and clarify our travel articles

We are also very grateful to the **London Greek Embassy Press & Communications Office** for their continuing support and to the **AG Leventis Foundation** for theirs.

Printed and bound by: JFDi Print Services Ltd in the UK

Greek-o-File Ltd, UK

Email: stc@greekofile.co.uk
Website: www.greekofile.co.uk
Telephone: +44 (0)1225 709907

Greek-o-File Volume 6 - Contents

Introduction

This year (2007) has been one of devastation from natural disasters and man-made tragedies in many parts of the world. Greece has had more than its share with the fires that have ravaged so much of their delicately balanced environment, killing more than sixty innocent victims.

Ours is not to judge nor blame - land-grabbing developers, overstretched government agencies struggling to cope with the scale of the problem, or the Greek people themselves for not caring enough about the ecological issues of the day, unthinkingly discarding lighted cigarettes or broken glass in tinderbox forests during one of the hottest, driest summers of recent times.

Commentators from inside and outside Greece have tried to find a culprit to accuse as vast swathes of the country attempt to recover and set about rebuilding livelihood, heritage, infrastructure and shattered dreams, not to mention dealing with the grief of lost loved ones.

As the Greek authorities worked hard for the immediate relief of the people affected and put forward ambitious plans for a top priority recovery of the areas ravaged, many grecophiles from around the world looked on in disbelief and despair at the scale of the disaster. They too have joined the efforts for relief and helping those who lost so much. Donations collected from ordinary people and aid distributed from government and charitable organisations will help in many practical ways.* EU-wide initiatives to establish rapid-response capabilities across member countries for all kinds of needs will provide faster and better help for the future.

Putting events back in proportion, although many areas suffered terribly, fortunately the vast majority of Greece was unscathed by the fires and hopefully lessons were learned to prevent devastation on the same scale again.

Through the pages of The Greek-o-File Volume 6 let us share, not just an enjoyment of the beauties and treasures of a land and people we've come to love, but also express our ongoing support for the Greek way of life. Cherish the experiences, live the fantasies, explore the yet-to-be-discovered places and people, knowing that even through the kind of adversity we've witnessed so recently, the heart-grabbing *filoxenia* and the unfettered kindness in Greece live on and continue to reach out with the warmest of welcomes.

Whether you leap through the book to devour every word as quickly as you can, or approach it slowly, returning again and again to savour each article, we hope the spirit of Greece shines through these pages to bring a little of that Hellenic heliotherapy to body, mind and soul.

Terry Cook

* A UK account has been set up for donations:- *Greek Embassy London, Fire Victims in Greece, Account no: 38859999, Sort Code: 40-62-04.*

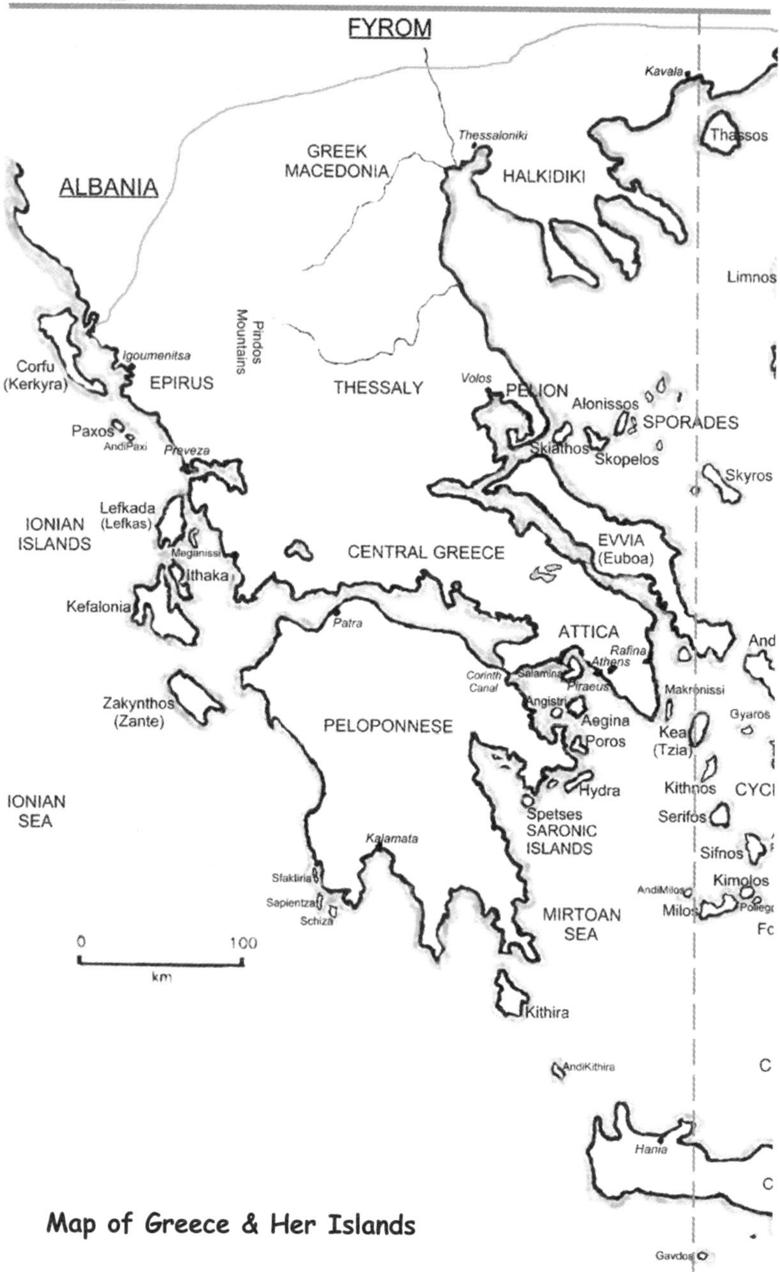

FYROM

<u>ALBANIA</u>

GREEK
MACEDONIA

Thessaloniki

HALKIDIKI

Kavala

Thassos

Limnos

Corfu
(Kerkyra)

Igoumenitsa

EPIRUS

Pindos
Mountains

THESSALY

Volos

PELION

Alonissos

SPORADES

Paxos
AndiPaxi

Preveza

Skiathos

Skopelos

Skyros

Lefkada
(Lefkas)

IONIAN
ISLANDS

Meganissi

Ithaka

CENTRAL GREECE

EVVIA
(Euboa)

Kefalonia

Patra

ATTICA

Rafina
Athens

And

Corinth
Canal

Salamina

Piraeus

Makronissi

Zakynthos
(Zante)

PELOPONNESE

Angistri

Aegina

Poros

Kea
(Tzia)

Gyaros

CYCL

IONIAN
SEA

Kalamata

Hydra

Kithnos

Spetses
SARONIC
ISLANDS

Serifos

Sifnos

Sfaktiria

Sapientza

Schiza

MIRTOAN
SEA

AndiMilos

Milos

Kimolos

Poliego

Fo

0   100

km

Kithira

AndiKithira

C

Hania

C

Map of Greece & Her Islands

Reference Map

Filoxenia - Welcome to Greece

As any regular visitor to Greece knows, 'φιλοξενία' (filoxenia) is the traditional Greek hospitality and friendliness (φίλος - friend) to strangers (ξένος - stranger, foreigner) that makes so many of us keep going back. Whether it be a friendly greeting as you walk by, a keenness to help you find what you are looking for, the little extras when you order food and drinks or just their 'way with words' they cannot fail to captivate your heart, your soul and your mind. This is the *essence* of the real Greece and the Greeks we love and miss when we are not there.

The following anecdotes of readers' experiences of *filoxenia* moments will strike a chord with many.

You Lead, I'll Follow *by Jane Stillwell*

One evening in late May in the small village of Elos, Western Crete, having been welcomed in to a taverna for a quick drink, it soon became apparent there was some sort of family celebration going on. Indeed my partner and I soon became involved with a local elderly Cretan gentleman's 90th birthday.

We were given raki, wine and birthday cake and I was even encouraged to have a dance with this lovely old character.

Now picture the scene ...

I am 5 foot 7 and fairly well endowed. The birthday boy was about 4 foot 10, so he had a big smile on his face and I felt as though a 'Benny Hill' sketch was in the making !!!

PLEASE Can We Have the Bill *by Jane Stillwell*

Before discovering Western Crete, my partner and I stayed many times in Elounda where a local Cretan, George, has rooms.

On one occasion on arrival we went to see George to pay for the week's rental of his apartment. Attempting to give George a handful of drachmas his response was *"No, no ... later, you pay me later."*

"But George, we want to pay you now in case we have no money left at the end of our holiday."

George replied, *"So if you spend the money, then this to me is no problem."*

The lovely thing being ... he meant it !

That's What Friends Are For *by Jackie Bott*

The beloved was struggling somewhat this year, owing to the fact he's awaiting a hip replacement operation, but he coped very well with the many steps down to and up from town at night, with the aid of his trusty walking stick.

As planned before we went to Skopelos, we met up with two fellow Greek-o-Filers on their second night there, just for 'a couple of drinks and a natter'. We were all a bit nervous at meeting for the first time, but soon hit if off, and the drinks and natter flowed. Parting company at around 4 am (not done that for many a year), we started to make our way back up to our apartment. (I have to say here in all honesty that although the drink had flowed, we were reasonably *compos mentis*.)

About half way home, the trusty stick let us down, catching in the cobbles, resulting in the beloved taking a nasty tumble. Prone on the ground, in shock, and neither moving nor speaking, he gave me a considerable scare. I finally got a mumble out of him, but unable in the dim light to tell if he'd broken anything, I admit to panicking a bit - and anyway, how was I going to get him back on his feet? He's a bit heavier than me.

Fortunately, we were in a street where we have some Greek friends, so I went and knocked on their door to get help, apologising profusely for the late hour.

Myrsini came to the door in her little yellow T-shirt top pyjamas, accompanied by her mother resplendent in full length nightgown, pink hairnet, and no teeth. Myrsini awoke Philip, who came out clad from head to foot in paisley winceyette pyjamas, and asked me if Alan was drunk. I said *"No",* which was the truth, just that he'd fallen because of his bad hip. Philip peered up the street, and we saw that Al was now back on his feet - thank God. I apologised again and thanked them for their support. They said *"No problem".*

I managed to get Al home, very slowly. He just had cuts and bruises, but it had been scary. Feeling really guilty at dragging our friends out of bed at such a late hour, we went over to see Philip at their out-of-town apartments a few days later, and spent some time chatting and drinking coffee with him. He appreciated that, and assured us that it hadn't been a problem and *"that's what friends are for".* We were extra careful after that, but it was also an unexpected insight to Greek summer nightwear - bearing in mind that it was 35°C during the day!

Savvas the Fisherman *by Pauline Hinson*

- Extracts from a Diary

Arriving on Leros, we had decided exactly where we wanted to stay in Alinda, but had not bargained on meeting Savvas with the other 'Rooms to let' people meeting the ferry. He had a sign 'Rooms on Alinda Beach'. We told him the name of the studios we wanted and he asked if we had booked, did they know we were coming?

We told him *"No, but we think we will like it there."*

"Why you want go there? Look across bay. I am right on the beach. Other place is further along road, up hill, 7-8 minutes to beach!"

"What is your place like then?" We wavered.

"You will have a big room, air conditioning, full kitchen - €25 per night."

"Mmm, sounds alright. Has it got a private balcony?"

"Yes, yes."

"Can we see the sea?"

"Yes, yes, yes." He'd hooked us.

"Alright. We will come and look at it."

Of course he landed us. We fell in love with it. The room was exactly as he said - about 15 metres back from the beach, a corner balcony overlooking the sea on one side and the garden on the other. Great for sitting out in the evening watching the lights coming on, illuminating the castle and Ag. Marina across the bay.

Savvas' garden and view across the bay

We went to see the other place later. He was right. It would have taken Gordon half an hour to go to the bakery in the morning for our fresh bread.

Savvas told us he was also a fisherman (of fish!). *"If you want fish one night - tell me."* We often saw him sitting on a plastic crate in the garden, gutting fish, so after a while we decided to take him up on his fish offer. He took us to his store room and put four grey and black striped fish, about 9 inches long, complete with heads, into a carrier bag.

He must have seen the expression on my face *"What do I do with them?"* as I'm more used to cooking prepared fish fillets back home.

"I am also a good cook," he declared. *"I'll bring them up to your room in half an hour."*

That was a relief. I smiled my acceptance of his kind offer.

We went up, cooked some rice, prepared our salad and opened a bottle of wine. Savvas brought the fish to us on a pretty plate, cooked to perfection and served with wedges of lemon.

"How much do we owe you?" we enquired. *"Nothing, just enjoy."*

What a lovely man he is. We did as instructed and really did 'enjoy' them.

Theo's Turn *by Tony Brown*

Whilst working one summer in a Greek kitchen (see p.133), one evening a couple came by who'd been in the previous evening and spent a small fortune. They asked if it was OK to sit at a table outside, but just for a couple of lemonades. Unusually, Theo was delighted, showed them to a table with a clear view of the street and served them himself. When they came to pay the bill, he said, *"Please, it's my turn. You paid last night."*

One More for the Road *by Jane Stillwell*

My dear friend John had never been to Greece before, so my partner and I invited him to Crete with us. We spent the days showing him the beautiful scenery and drove up to a plateau via an extremely twisty road with one double bend after another - so the taverna at the top looked rather inviting.

We had a light lunch - Greek salad and all the trimmings - and as is usual in Crete we were offered free raki. John had not even tasted ouzo before, so his first sip was truly baptism by fire !

John declined another glass but to no avail, with the friendly Cretan owner proclaiming *"Drink, drink ... this is good for you. Kala, kala ... it will make the road straight."*

"Please, You Come Again" *by Roy Lawrance*

We sat like inmates from a lunatic asylum, smiling inanely at each other, the dozen or so words we knew of each other's language soon exhausted. Only the cat seemed truly relaxed and didn't appear to have moved since our visit last year.

Every year it was the same, *"Please, come for coffee"* and every year it was the same predictable outcome of polite inevitable silence.

A sudden flash of inspiration from my wife broke the void.

"No fish?" she said pointing to the empty goldfish bowl that for the last few years had been home to 'Scorpios', who's growth rate had out-matched his turning circle and left us wondering last year if he was actually wedged in.

"Ah ... Scorpios" said Dimitri's wife, whose name we never remember and have to mumble, sprang to her feet religiously crossing herself and began searching through the pile of debris on the window sill.

"Him dead" she said, proudly waving the skeletal dried remains of the fish like some deceased relative.

I've never quite understood the fascination Greeks have with death, or come to terms with how they deal with the bodies of the deceased.

My bored eyes scanned the room. This year, the windows all had new wooden pelmets over them, held in place by nailed telephone cable clips, which were much quicker than screws, except that one was on the floor alongside a lump of broken plaster. These pelmets were clearly the must-have items in Sigri this year, as many of the houses now sported them. They came in two sizes - those that were far too wide for the windows and those that were too narrow. In many cases, they were fixed low enough to make it impossible to fully open the windows any more, and with the arrival of the spirit level in the average home still being a way off, they made for an interesting make-over.

In the corner of the room was an ultraviolet electric fly zapper, that at night provided amazing in-house lightening displays each time it claimed another victim. Greece's answer to the lava lamp; but with an ending!

More effective however, was the outside porch light which was crammed solid with many now-extinct species of moth. It was not until we set about cleaning ours out, back at the apartment, that we realised the light bulb inside was on, and had probably been so for many years.

"The museum is coming along though?" I continued.

"I not know, I too busy ... maybe I go next year?" Another pregnant pause.

"Today I went for a walk to Andromakis beach." I said in an attempt to break the silence.

"Andromakis ... I never go!" Dimitri said, as though I was referring to some remote part of Tibet that was yet to be mapped.

"Never?" I exclaimed.

"No ... is too far ... what I go for?"

As a child growing up here, I would have been there every day, but then I am not Greek, and maybe our comparatively overcrowded island makes us want to explore these remote places.

For these annual visits we always bring a present which is always gratefully received but never opened in our presence, which does make it difficult to know if we are taking the right things. In return, when we leave, we are always given a jar of sticky preserve that we would dearly like to stop, but just cannot break the cycle.

In my search for conversation one year, I stupidly pointed to a hand-crocheted table decoration and said, *"That's nice, did you make it?"*

Instantly it was rolled up and presented to us, despite our protests, with its great grandmother's origins explained in mime. It's hideous, but we refer to it each visit with great affection, though I'm convinced they were secretly glad to see the back of it.

As luck would have it, just as the sticky spoons of glacéd cherries appeared, the 'Punch and Judy' speakers of the mobile 'knicker van' crackled outside in the street, and the room emptied. We fol-
lowed them out to inspect what was on offer, leaving three spoons sticking out of our daughter's mouth. To be honest, some of the items were now coming back into fashion and quite trendy in a 60's sort of way, but these mobile vans, bringing fruit, vegetables, clothes and live
chickens, are still the lifeblood of many small villages like Sigri in Western Lesvos. Supermarkets are making an appearance but are considered far too expensive by the old and staff seem incapable of pointing to the appropriate euro coins that they have no understanding of. In such tightknit communities with everyone looking out for each other, buying condoms is definitely something you would do in another village and even then the news will probably beat you home.

Avoiding returning to the house, we said our goodbyes, each as relieved it was all over. We headed towards Yiannis' for a late lunch before the beach.

"Please, you come again" Dimitris shouted as we turned the corner.

Tales of Greek Healthcare

Not for the first time, we received stories of medical problems experienced and expertly dealt with whilst in Greece. The Greek healthcare system is different from ours and these differences need to be understood - but first some reader experiences.

Good Timing for a Bad 'Trip' *by Chris Duckworth*

In May 2006 my husband, Bernard, and I arrived on the island of Lipsi for our annual visit - our sixth time on this lovely island.

On the second day, I arose early for my usual morning run. I was almost back at our apartment when I caught my foot in some concrete reinforcing wire and sprawled headlong onto my knees. A passing motorcyclist helped me up, but feeling foolish and shaken, I thanked him and limped back to our apartment dripping blood. Bernard was quite shocked to see me all splattered with blood. What I had not realised was that a metal spike had pierced and split my ear leaving a piece hanging down like an earring.

I cleaned myself up, then held a pad to my ear. Bernard called our Laskarina island manager, Sally. She contacted the doctor who lived above the local surgery/health centre and arranged to meet us there at 8.30 am. When we arrived Sally and the doctor were quite shocked at the extent of my injury. After examining it, the doctor said she was unable to stitch the wound. With Sally's Greek and doctor's assistant Kosmina's English we were able to communicate quite well and I understood that they believed the torn flesh on my ear was deteriorating fast and appeared beyond redemption. She would have to cut out the torn strip, leaving a gap and I would need to go to Athens for plastic surgery. As you can imagine I was horrified. Bernard had been ill before our holiday and was looking forward to rest and relaxation, the last thing we wanted was to travel to Athens and lose a chunk of holiday (not to mention a chunk of ear!).

At this point the gods smiled on me. Kosmina remembered that a group of doctors had arrived on the island the day before as part of their annual convention. They had been out the evening before, celebrating after the Greek Minister of Health had laid the Foundation Stone for a new health centre on Lipsi, and were due to leave for Patmos that afternoon.

Whilst waiting to find out if they could help, the receptionist, Voula, produced a cake which we all shared and many phone calls later one of the doctors arrived at the surgery. To our astonishment, he was a plastic surgeon from Athens, named Koutos Parastenas. He took one look at my ear and said he could stitch it. He produced a medical bag complete with scalpels, sutures, gown, etc, gave me a local anaesthetic and set to work. The facilities were rather basic and a little ramshackle with other patients coming in and out, but despite all this the surgeon made a wonderful job, putting in 16 neat stitches.

Following an anti tetanus injection and a prescription for antibiotics, the plastic surgeon was giving me instructions on caring for my injury when

Summer waiting room

he noticed that one of my knees had also suffered from the fall and had swollen quite badly. They disinfected and cleaned the wound and put ice packs on the joint. He thought there may be a problem, made more phone calls and another surgeon arrived to look at my knee. She said she did not think it was serious but would like a colleague to look. Voula and Kosmina rang round again to track down an orthopaedic surgeon who soon arrived. I was advised to go to Leros for an x-ray, as I may have cracked the patella.

We went to the tour operator's office where their local agent, Rena, told us there was a catamaran leaving for Leros at 1 pm. The Laskarina agent on Leros, Michaelis, would meet the boat, organise a taxi to take us to the hospital and explain that I needed to catch the last boat, the 4 pm Flying Dolphin, back to Lipsi, or arrange overnight accommodation if needed.

We had a quick lunch, collected overnight gear and caught the boat. As arranged, Michaelis met us and followed us to the hospital. Apparently it normally closed at 2 pm but the surgery in Lipsi had rung ahead and the radiographer and doctor agreed to remain to see me. I had three x-rays that fortunately were normal. Michaelis organised a taxi back to the harbour in time to catch the Dolphin back to Lipsi.

A few days later I visited the Lipsi doctor who redressed the ear and on a subsequent visit removed most of the stitches. The last three, in the cartilage, were removed at the health centre back home where they were impressed at the neat stitches and lack of scarring.

What could have been a disaster, but for fortuitous circumstances and the dedicated good will of all involved, had very little negative impact on our holiday. Sally, Rena and Michaelis, the plastic surgeon, doctors and Greek medical system all gave such excellent service for which my ear and I remain sincerely grateful.

A Tale of Two Healthcare Systems *by Peter Stoneley*

It was 14th June, two days before my 72nd birthday and I was being cuddled by the buxom 70 year old widow from across the road. Aleka was calling out softly *"Oh, Petros, Petros, oh Petros."* She had my arms pinned down across my chest and I struggled to move. Blood was everywhere. Desperate to raise a hand to shield my face from the sun, I tried to call out, but only groans and moans came. Convinced it was some strange dream my consciousness slipped away as she cried out loudly: *"Natasha, Natasha, Ela!"*.

Mumbling voices stirred me. I couldn't move but managed to open one eye to see Homeros holding a multi coloured beach umbrella to shade my head. Doctor Yannis was pacing up and down. He peered into my one working eye and stuck his finger into the other. I slipped away again.

The clatter of the stretcher trolley over the stonework persuaded the other eye to open and Natasha and I were soon in the ambulance on our way to Corfu General Hospital. My head hurt and my memory was juggling with what little pieces of information it could find. Natasha reminded me that we had taken coffee to the beach, but a cold wind had driven us off, back home for lunch. While I went to shut the gates she had gone indoors and had been wondering where I was when she heard Aleka calling. Aleka had rushed over to find me covered in blood from a head wound after her granddaughter said I was lying outside our gates. Assuming that I had fallen and hit my head on the low stone wall, she tried to make me comfortable and called out for Natasha. Homeros was passing on his motor scooter and went off to get Dr Yannis from his surgery. He thought my head needed stitches and called the ambulance.

It felt like a team of wrestlers were pulling pieces of my head together with pliers whilst others were using steel wire to make stitches and lump hammers to flatten the whole thing down. The back of my head hurt. A man in a white coat asked me why I had fallen but I didn't know. He asked if I had any chest pains and seemed surprised that I didn't. He frowned, *"You have a headache then."* It was as much a statement as a question.

Absurd as it sounds, I said *"No, I don't have a headache but my head aches."*

"And no pains in the chest?"

"No"

"None at all?"

"No"

After whispering in the corner, two men helped me from the trolley and onto a wheelchair. *"We will take some x-rays if that is OK with you?"* Courteous and polite as ever, they wheeled me off and took two head and one chest x-rays. Then on to the neurologist, who hammered several joints and told me to watch his blurred finger. On to the cardiologist where there was a bit of a hold up. He apologised for the delay, looked at the x-rays and the neurologist's report, took an ECG and asked if I had any pains in the chest. *"No? Really? A headache then?"*

My refusal to admit to any pain other than the stitched area at the back of my head earned me a bed in the cardiology ward upstairs. The first thing they wanted was my European Health Insurance Card. At least that made them happy!

The two other beds were occupied by elderly men, their wives sitting on hard plastic chairs at the ends of their beds. In this hospital there is no nursing as we know it. Nursing care is provided by relatives, often working in shifts. Meals are provided for the patients but not for their relatives, so Natasha snacked on yoghurts and rolls from the kiosk outside and spent an uncomfortable night on a hard chair.

In the morning, after the same *"Chest pain? Headache?"* question and answer routine, they fitted me up with an ECG machine which I had to wear for 24 hours - another uncomfortable night for Natasha !

The cardiologist, a dapper chap with a fine black moustache and goatee beard, was unhappy with the 24 hour ECG and wanted more tests. He spoke very little English and my Greek was struggling with the medical references. In the afternoon I was taken down into the basement for a CT scan, then back up to a walking machine where a shy young trainee was instructed in how to wire me up. Her giggling did not help my mood after two nights virtually without sleep.

After 5 minutes staggering about on the walking machine I was puffing hard. The dapper little doctor smiled grimly and asked if I found breathing difficult.

"I am 72" I said, suddenly realising that it was my birthday. *"I'm allowed!"*.

He then did an echo test. After studying all the results, he told me that he thought I needed a little machine to keep my heart beating in rhythm. I realised he was talking about a pacemaker. I would have to go to Ioanina, 100 km up into the mountains on the Greek mainland, or I could go back to the UK for treatment. I spent most of the night pacing the balcony and let the old chap's wife have my bed. A tall doctor had taken pity on Natasha and pushed a spare bed into the corridor for her.

It was now Saturday morning. I found the dapper doctor, signed a release form, and was presented with a discharge form and copies of the reports of all the tests. By midday we were outside at the kiosk sipping coffee in the warm sun, waiting for a taxi home. The rest of the weekend was spent pottering, relaxing in the garden and pondering. This appeared to be a serious warning - the red card ! The ouzo bottle remained untouched.

Our insurers had validated our 'claim' at the first phone call, but now they wanted all the hospital reports faxed to them. Noticing that there was a cardiologist above the bookshop with the fax machine, I went in on impulse for a second opinion.

He did an ECG, pored over the read-outs and reports and told me that there was a minor heart problem which was not serious enough to make me fall but needed investigation. The next step in finding why I fell would be an ultra sound check on the carotid arteries and then an MRI brain scan.

Early that evening, I had what can only be described as an epileptic-type fit, followed by another in the early hours of the morning - so perhaps Aleka had been restraining me, not cuddling me as I thought I had dreamed. Dr. Yannis came and he called Dimitris the cardiologist, by which time I was conscious again and lucid. Blood pressure and pulse were OK. They both felt that it would pass and I should go back to the UK to see my own doctor. Natasha phoned the insurers to bring them up to date. Their medical team promptly rang back to say that I may not be well enough to travel and should have the carotid artery check.

So Tuesday morning, we took the village taxi to Corfu Town to see a radiologist. Surprised to find the walls of his office completely covered with paintings we chatted for a while, learned that he had taken up painting to keep his hands occupied after giving up smoking; haggled over the price of a delightful picture of the fishing boats in Petriti harbour and eventually settled to the ultrasound artery test which he pronounced average for a man of my age and nothing there to cause the fits we described. He suggested the next step should be the neurologist just around the corner and an MRI.

The neurologist prescribed anti clotting medication and an anti convulsion pill to reduce the effects of the seizures as a temporary measure in order to get me back to the UK for an MRI.

The insurer's medical team then insisted on arranging for a doctor to accompany us home, so we had to wait for them to book flights to fit in with an available doctor. By Saturday the pills were enjoying their side effects and I couldn't think straight. Walking was becoming progressively more difficult. I had a sore throat and breathing was difficult.

Dr Yannis came on Wednesday to remove the stitches. Natasha made coffee which he drank whilst smoking a cheroot and talking politics. Natasha teased him, asking how he reconciled smoking with being a doctor. *"My dear,"* he said *"I am a doctor, not a saint."*

On Saturday our return was confirmed with a 3 pm call from the insurers and at 10 pm Dr Athena arrived; young, attractive, long flowing hair, eye lashes to match and "PRETTY BABE" emblazoned across her T-shirt. I was wheezing and feeling my age. She would return at 5 am in the morning to take us to the airport for the 7 am flight to Athens.

Doctor and patient settled themselves comfortably in business class. Natasha was in the economy seats somewhere behind us. Dr Athena was splendid; she sweet talked the flight attendant into letting Natasha join us, connected me up to the oxygen supply and we all sat and chatted. On the Athens to Heathrow flight she did her best, but my wife had to eat her economy lunch before she could join us in business class. Athena spoke excellent English, organised a wheelchair and whizzed us through the formalities at Heathrow and out to the waiting taxi hired by the insurers.

We already had flights booked for our autumn trip so I decided to 'go private' to speed things up. Even paying privately it was not possible to see a cardiologist quickly and when we did he found nothing wrong. The neurologist looked at the Greek handwritten medical reports upside down and said that I had hardening of the arteries and should continue with the temporary medication prescribed by the Greek neurologist. He was adamant that an MRI scan would not give us any different information. Also I should not drive until I was free from convulsions for a year and should surrender my driving licence.

So I gave up my licence, sold the car and went back to Corfu in September still feeling the worse for the medication. Balance and coordination were big problems, my stomach was in disarray and grumpiness had set in.

Our elder daughter, Holly, had booked to come with us for the first 10 days, so she drove us around - for five days that is, until I had another seizure in the middle of the night and woke everyone up with my moaning. Dr Yannis came; he called Dr Dimitris who called the ambulance after he had taken my almost nonexistent pulse and declared *"He needs a pacemaker - NOW."*

 There are three days missing from my memory but Natasha and Holly tell me that I had periods when I was awake and talking as if nothing had happened. At Corfu General Hospital I was put on a monitor and they spent the night watching my pulse reading fluctuate between 35 and 40. In the morning they squeezed us all into an ambulance to transfer us to Ioanina. In the vehicle hold of the ferry the temperature rose to 34°C but I was happily flirting with the nurse who had just been instructed in the use of the resuscitation shock paddles and was looking very nervous. At Ioanina Uni-

versity Hospital my operation was scheduled for early the following morning, so being early evening the girls went off to find food in a pleasant restaurant in the hospital. On their way back they were met by the doctor who had admitted us and were told that my condition had deteriorated, forcing them to fit the pacemaker immediately and I was now back in my room.

I was discharged the next day but I have no memory of any instructions or how we got home. The next morning I woke up. *"What happened?"*

Holly had two more days driving her semi-demented father around before jetting off back to England and her work. We settled down to a month of relaxation and walking. On the eighth day we walked to Ringlathes where Dr Dimitris took the stitches out and declared everything was working OK. I felt good.

We did what we could in the garden, got the bamboos cut down as there were about thirty flower spikes reaching 16 or more feet into the air, waving into the telephone cables. Aleka kindly said she would take half for her garden and quickly gathered up one end of the heap. Tucking them under her arm she marched off across the road, dragging the poles behind her. I ran and scooped up the other end to help her across the road and into her drive. By the time we had reached her gates my heart was thumping like a steam hammer and I was gasping for breath; my face felt red hot and flushed but the rest of me felt like a wet rag hung out to drip dry. I had to sit down.

When the time came to go back to Ioanina for my checkup we travelled the day before and booked into a hotel to give ourselves plenty of time. Ioanina is a lively, attractive lakeside city with a holiday atmosphere about it; tavernas, bars, ice cream parlours, sweet shops and jewellery shops line the streets and waterfront; and the local population turns out for the evening *volta* to see and to be seen.

The spacious entrance of the hospital houses a large canteen, a small information desk and rows of counters where queues of people sit clutching their numbered tickets and waiting their turn. All the signs are in Greek, but 'cardiology' is a Greek word. At the end of a long corridor we found

Church at Ioanina University Hospital

the ward and a door marked 'IATPOI' (doctors).

"Your surgeon is at home ill today," said the white coated young lad who opened the door just wide enough to see our appointment paper. *"Go back to the main entrance and ask for the clinic."*

At the clinic we pulled a numbered slip from a machine, waited for our number to come up, showed my European Insurance Card, registered, and were directed to another queue to pay €3 for our visit. At the clinic all twenty or so seats were occupied and most of the passageway was blocked by people standing looking at the floor. A nurse took my papers, made a note and signalled me to wait outside. It seemed I had to wait my turn, but each time the door opened to let a patient out, there was a rush and the doorway was blocked. It looked as if only the fittest got to see the doctor ! All the Greeks had an able-bodied and fast relative with them to do their barging. It took an hour to get ourselves a seat next to the door so I could leap up at the crucial moment.

Surprised to find a foreigner at his clinic, the doctor introduced himself as Spiros Papas. He placed something on my chest over the pacemaker, watched the machinery and decided everything was working properly. I asked if I would know when the pacemaker cut in and told him about Aleka and the bamboo.

"You will not know when it starts," he paused, looking me up and down, *"or when it stops."* He consulted the papers, nodding slowly : *"You are over 70. It's time to stop chasing women!"*

But I feel fitter now than I have felt for years !

The six Greek doctors I saw, (including Athena) all believed that my convulsions were caused by a heart problem. I believe the Greeks saved my life.

Helpful Notes

Before you travel to Greece

1) Get a European Health Insurance Card. It is free and your policy may be invalid without it. *Having this card meant no charge was made for ambulances, hospital bed, meals (patient only), tests, operation, pacemaker itself and the checkup.*

2) Check exactly what your insurance policy covers.

3) If you have an annual policy, have you declared any changes in your health since it commenced? It may be invalid if you haven't. *Mine cost £150 to continue after the June episode. I have yet to find out what the extra will be now !*

and in the event of medical problems :

4) Have plenty of spare cash with you - you may get it back but will need receipts for everything. In particular, taxis should always carry receipt pads

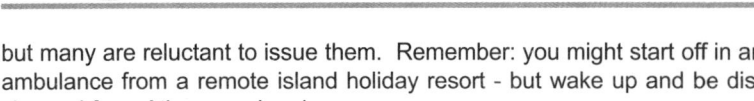

but many are reluctant to issue them. Remember: you might start off in an ambulance from a remote island holiday resort - but wake up and be discharged from Athens, or Ioanina.

5) Doctors rarely carry receipts on call-outs. You may have to visit the surgery later to get one. Expect to pay a minimum €30 for a visit, more for something like removing stitches, double that for specialists eg. cardiologist or neurologist. *We paid for all taxis including getting home from both hospitals and getting to Ioanina for the checkup, ferry crossings, local doctor, local cardiologist, additional tests required by insurers by radiologist and neurologist and their fees. In total it cost us around £500 in June, most of which we got back from insurers; and around £400 in September (£300 of which was taxis).*

6) I have deliberately not mentioned the 'little brown envelopes' I have heard about as I got by without them.

7) It is imperative to keep insurers informed and to follow their advice or insurance will be invalid. Their medical care is superb - regular phone calls to check, advice, etc.

Re language: Amazingly, in most cases the Greek medical people we encountered found it easier to understand my awful Greek than I did to understand their English. The only exception was Dr Athena - her English is superb (we are still in touch). It was difficult enough as it was; without any Greek it would have been a nightmare.

If you would like to discuss any matters arising from this, please leave a message in the guest book on my web site www.PeterStoneley-onCorfu.co.uk

- See also book reviews for Peter's earlier experiences in Greece p165.

Another Visit to the Pharmacist *by Jackie Bott*

Improvisation is very much the name of the game while we're on holiday - we take as much stuff as we can with us to cover all eventualities and this year I thought we were covered. Not a bit of it ! I woke up one morning with a horrendous swelling on my inner left thigh. Never seen anything like it. A particularly nasty bite of some description, the 3 inch patch had a ring of white round it, and looked like some kind of allergic reaction.

A visit to the pharmacist saw a 4-day treatment plan devised and put into operation. We have used the pharmacy on previous visits, so we know they are able to offer treatment for many minor ailments. Ointment was prescribed, to be put on 3 times a day, with some steroid tablets to be taken at varying frequencies.

The 'no dairy or fish' in the plan was a bit of a problem. Have you ever studied a Greek menu and tried

to order a meal without cheese, milk or butter in it? Well, most of MY favourites have cheese of some description tucked away in them somewhere. That meant the customary breakfast omelette, along with the ice-creams and yoghourt also went out of the window for a few days.

'No soap to be used in shower or washing' was a bit difficult, with selective area washing and shampooing then taking place followed by strategically placed applications of aftersun lotion. But the worst one was being instructed 'no exposure of the offending limb to the sun'. We managed to get round it by putting one of hubby's big white hankies, neatly folded to the correct size, over the swollen area while sunbathing, tied on with a shoelace, and very fetching it looked too - the perfect accessory.

All was well after a couple of return visits to the pharmacist for checkups, and the all-clear to resume normal activities was finally given, when we called in on our way out to dinner 4 days later.

The final comment that evening as we set out for the evening was *"mmm, nice skirt"* - and yes, it did have a petti underneath it ! (ref. Vol 5 p 32)

And Another ...

The Chemist/Pharmacy gets better by the year. Last year's giant leg bite is just a memory and the lovely girl who saw me through its treatment has moved on. This time I confronted the pharmacist with a horrendous upper left arm, plastered with bright red pustules - my body's reaction to 40 - 44°C of heat.

"Ne, ne, ne" said he *"just a few moments - sit please"* Not being one to argue, I did as I was told and watched the stream of people calling in:- girl with foot in plaster, girl with chipped nail varnish, furtive man, another furtive man - and so on.

My prescription finally arrived. A *"specially made for you"* potion, knocked up in the back of the shop, *"with vitamin"* for extra effectiveness. I was presented with a large pot of paste - complete with a large lolly-pop stick, instructions to apply it liberally three times a day, and told to keep it in the fridge in the meantime.

On my first application of this wonder cream, the beloved instantly recognised it. *"Looks like polyfiller,"* said he. We did our best to comply, but ... have you ever tried to spread really cold paste over some part of your anatomy, in Greece, with a lolly-pop stick? It was quite hilarious.

I did as I was told and my arm soon improved and settled down.

Don't you just know it though, now back in the UK the same arm itches to distraction again. Now then, where is that pot of paste? Maybe lurking at the back of the fridge? Must be around here somewhere ...

Medical Cover in Greece - Current Facts *by Sylvia Cook*

Not much has changed since our report in Volume 2. To summarise with the latest information from Dept. of Health and Dept. for Work & Pensions:

As **a holidaymaker** you need a European Health Insurance Card (EHIC). The old E111 replaced in Jan 2006 is now invalid. The quickest way to get one is on-line from www.ehic.org.uk. It covers you for state provided medical treatment throughout Europe for trips up to a **maximum of 13 weeks**. You will be treated on the same basis as a local state-insured person, which may not be the same as the UK NHS (eg. you may have to contribute to the cost of your care, pay for drugs prescribed, and nursing care if available).

The EHIC does cover regular treatment for chronic or preexisting diseases, but you may need to make arrangements in advance for items such as oxygen - call **DoH Customer Service Centre 020 7210 4850** for details. You are not covered if you knowingly go abroad for specific treatment, but, if you are going to Greece expecting to have a baby there, you will need to take form E112 with supporting details with you.

Travel or health insurance is needed to cover other costs, see examples in Peter Stoneley's article and 'Helpful Notes'.

If you go to **work in Greece** for up to a year and **continue paying UK national insurance** you can apply for a UK EHIC valid for the period you work there, for yourself and your dependants. For longer than a year check with HM Revenue and Customs. If working for a Greek company or self employed in Greece you will need to pay contributions to the Greek IKA system for a while before being entitled to a Greek issued EHIC. There are variations for students, nannies and au pairs.

A UK issued EHIC is not applicable if you are **going to live and not work** in Greece, or spend **more than 6 months** there in any year. If you are **under the UK state pension age** contact the UK **Department for Work (0191 218 1999)** who can tell you whether or not the UK will fund any medical treatment if required in Greece and for how long. You may be able to get health cover financed by the UK on form E106 for a limited period (1 to 1.75 years), generally if you have paid NI for at least the previous two years on earnings over the threshold (about £4500 for tax year 2007/8).

If you go to live in Greece and are receiving a UK **state retirement pension** or UK social security benefit, you will need form E121 to apply for a Greek IKA card entitling you to cheaper drugs and full Greek medical services.

If you reside **outside the UK more than 6 months**, even if you are paying UK tax on your income and investments, you are NOT entitled to UK NHS care on return trips (unfair but true), other than for emergency treatment, so make sure you have the relevant E-form BEFORE you travel.

Aeolus Harnessed & 'Green' Energy *by Sylvia Cook*

Ever since Homer wrote of Aeolus trapping the winds in a goatskin bag, Greeks have appreciated not only the power of the wind, but the advantages of harnessing that power.

According to Homer, Aeolus was charged with looking after the winds by the gods, and could release them at will to help or hinder mankind. Aeolus was later known as the god of the wind. In the original story he also invented ships' sails - the first real use of the power of the winds, exploited extensively in ancient and modern Greece. Even today Greece is one of the most idyllic places to 'catch the wind in your sails' for novices and expert sailors alike.

Although the watermill was invented in Greece around 450BC, it seems the windmill took a little longer to arrive. Some sources say the windmill was invented 300BC by Egyptians and Greeks with *"8-10 wooden beams, rigged with sails and a rotor that turned perpendicular to the wind direction'"*, others say the Persians invented the windmill in 634AD, but it wasn't until the Crusaders returned in the 12th century that windmill technology was brought to Europe.

What is known is that Venetian engineers designed the windmill powered irrigation system on Crete's Lassithi plateau in the 1400's and that windmills, of the types we now often see derelict, were extensively used for irrigation and for milling grain throughout Greece, right through to the mid 20th century when electricity and oil power were able to provide so much more.

Wind is a large body of air moving rapidly and naturally, created by the uneven heating of the earth's surface. As a mountainous land surrounded by sea and rocky islands, wind is a natural asset to Greece in these days of encouraging environmentally friendly energy sources.

It wasn't until the late 1800's in Denmark that windmills were first used to produce electricity, rather than raw mechanical power. Modern windmills

which started to spring up around Greece late 1970 to 80's are more accurately called wind turbines and convert wind energy to electricity. Wind farms, or wind parks, are where several of these are grouped in places where high winds are likely and the electricity is transferred to the electricity grid for distributed use. The mountain and hill ridges where you now see rows of modern wind turbines gently turning are not so different from the ridges on which rows of windmills were built centuries ago to mill grain or carry water - like these, now renovated for show only, outside Serifos Hora, or at Olymbos, Karpathos *(previous page)*.

With the demand for electricity in Greece growing faster than much of the rest of Europe (the per capita consumption in Greece is currently lower than the European average), this modern wind-power technology is of obvious importance as the world tries to reduce its dependence on fossil fuels. Current wind power output in Greece is already about 500 megawatts and will increase to 2,000 Mw with planned installations by 2010.

The Centre for Renewable Energy Sources claims Greece could provide 15% of its energy from wind farms and 30% from solar power. Other renewable energy sources such as biomass gases (bioethanol & biodiesel from plants), and hydro electric power make small contributions in Greece too. New renewable energy sources are also being assessed, such as a geothermal power plant which has been approved on Lesvos.

This land of sunshine has obviously not been slow to harness the heat of the sun too. In simpler times, storing water in a (usually black plastic) water butt on the roof, or elsewhere exposed to the sun, was sufficient to provide warm to hot water for showers and cleaning on a sunny day. Today Greece is the second country in Europe for use of 'solar collectors' per capita. Most of this is in the form of low cost solar water heaters, which save the need for electricity to heat water for much of the year in many homes and in tourist accommodation. About 1 million Greek homes now provide 80% of their annual hot water supply with solar heaters. As this technology has improved over the years, some solar heaters can provide sufficient heat, or enough to significantly minimise electrical top up, to heat homes in the cooler months too.

Photovoltaic (PV) technology converts light to electricity via solar cells. A small cell could be used to power equipment or to recharge a battery, but the first large-scale application of photovoltaics was to power orbiting satellites and spacecraft. Now it is being used for grid connected power generation and in some cases for remote homes.

Greece is investing heavily in photovoltaics and although PV is often privately installed, the 50 Mw PV park planned for Crete in 2006 was the first large grid-connected system in Greece and even the tiny southerly island of Gavdos will have a 100 Kilowatt PV installation. To understand the capacity and impact, compare this with the recently released news (Aug 2007) that an 8 Mw PV Park to be built on 15 acres southeast of Athens' E. Venizelos Airport will supply 30% of the airport's total power requirement in 2 years time, and a 33 Kw unit installed on the roof of a German school in Athens in 2004 was predicted to save over 24 tons of carbon dioxide emissions each year.

Greece is making a very real effort to reduce its 'carbon footprint' by significant use of renewable energy sources. Harnessing the natural powers of wind and sun will help protect the Earth, by replacing power produced more conventionally which pollutes the atmosphere with greenhouse gases, dangerous carbon monoxide, sulphur dioxide and cancer causing microscopic particles. It's got to be good for us all and I for one am happy to see today's elegant windmills gracing our Lesvos hilltops.

It's a Dogs' Life *by Rudi Clarke*

*Claire and Paul Clarke's 1-year old black labrador/
collie cross came with them in February 2007 for a
sabbatical to try out a new life in Greece. Aided by
Claire he penned a letter to her brother's children back
home in England, adapted below.*

Dear Rosie, Tom & Ben,

Well ... a lot has happened since I saw you all at
Christmas. We've been on a long, long road
trip; me in my 'travel crate' in the back of Paul
and Claire's car, surrounded by all sorts of other
things they thought they might need in this place. We went through the
Channel Tunnel and on to Belgium - I've even got my own passport now!

First we visited your aunty and cousins in Holland, but only stayed one night
before going through Belgium and Luxembourg to stop in France at a place
called Longwee (which is just what I needed on arrival). I like the French
because they like me. They had a special price of just €5 for dogs to stay
with people in the hotel. Next day we drove on and the weather turned very
strange. We stopped at a service station where everything was covered in
white stuff - called 'snow' they said. I've not seen anything like it before, but
it was very cold to stand on and I couldn't see the grass or bushes to wee on
- very confusing.

We travelled on to 'the South of France' which turned out to be a very smart
hotel in Juan Les Pins. We planned to stay 2 days so we could all stretch
our legs after all that travelling. I loved running along the beach and seeing
the boats in nearby Antibes. As luck would have it, the car didn't want to
leave either and refused to start. It got towed away by a big truck - and
being a Friday could not be fixed for a few days. We ended up staying there
another 4 days. The receptionist and I were delighted as we'd struck up
quite a friendship by then. I was welcomed in all the restaurants and generally made a fuss of - even got my own plate of meat at my favourite place.

Driving through the next country, Italy, was not such fun - lots of tunnels and
bridges and at the end of the day it was difficult to find a hotel that was open.
Eventually we found a grotty one. Fortunately I had some food, but poor
Paul and Claire went to bed with nothing to eat because they don't eat my
food. We set off early next morning to get to a port, Ancona, where we
boarded a big ferry for nearly a day at sea to get to our new country.

Dogs aren't allowed inside the boat so I was shown to a kennel outside at
the top of the boat. I didn't like the look of it at all. Claire walked me around

the deck to see if I wanted a wee, but there were no smells to encourage me and it was all a bit difficult. Claire didn't like the kennel area either, so they smuggled me into their cabin and I had to stay very quiet so nobody knew I was there. I tried my best, but the next morning someone knocked on our door to tell us we were arriving in Greece and I 'woofed'! The man looked very cross when Claire opened the door, but we'd arrived so it was too late. We thought we'd stay at Patras one night but it was difficult finding a hotel where I could stay too. Luckily we found a very nice 4-star hotel with tasteful wall paper - I showed my appreciation by eating a bit of it.

Next day we drove to another port, Piraeus, for another boat where they didn't seem to like me either. They wouldn't let me inside and I was put in a tiny cage on the top deck. Claire was very upset and told the man I was a champion dog worth a lot of money and if anything happened to me she would sue. I was impressed as I think I'm just an ordinary dog really.

There was another dog in a cage next to me. It was very cold and very windy so we just howled out for help. After about 2 hours when we were out at sea Claire and Paul came and rescued me. They wanted to rescue my neighbour too, but didn't know where her owners were so had to leave her in the cage. Again I had to hide in their cabin, but I was really good this time.

The journey was only supposed to be 12 hours, but the sea was very rough so we stopped a long time at another island called Chios and it was 24 hours before we got to our destination, Lesvos.

As we approached Mytilene, the capital town, I began to understand what the long journey had been for. The island looked beautiful - lots of green and hills with villages dotted about, beaches, rocky cliffs and the sea all around, then the busy port with big houses, little shops, busy people, interesting smells. We drove off the boat and after about an hour's driving stopped for a run on the beach at Skala Kalloni, which was great. Another hour later we arrived at the village square of Eresos, Paul and Claire's Greek village. They were very happy to arrive at last. Lots of people came to say 'hello', or 'yassou' and 'Kalimera' as the Greeks say.

Next on to my new home - a little house with a small courtyard - much smaller than I'm used to. When we got there I was introduced to another dog, a ginger coloured boxer called Billy. Apparently Paul and Claire met Billy last year whilst I was at 'boot camp' in Wales, learning how to be a good dog. Billy was found wandering all alone and not very well when he was a tiny puppy. He went to live at a place called 'The Sanctuary' which is a bit like an orphanage for dogs. All the dogs there want to be adopted by loving people. Billy couldn't believe his luck when he came to live with us. He is very funny. He can stand on his hind legs without any help, just like the people, and he always has a smile on his face.

Everyday things are all new to Billy and he gets very excited. I say *"Stay cool Bill"*, but he can't help himself. He can be a bit of a pain sometimes though, for example, if I go to Paul or Claire for a cuddle he buts in. We've started to call him 'Billy-but'.

I thought things were getting a bit out of hand when, only a few days after getting here, a girl dog joined us. She had been found wandering the streets with nowhere to go and there was no room at The Sanctuary, so, guess what, she moved in with us. We called her Lady, but she didn't behave like one! She was so used to scavenging for food that she would tip the kitchen bin over and make such a mess. She also ate the back of our car seat. Eventually they had room for Lady at The Sanctuary, so we said our good-byes. We drive past and wave to her every day on our way to the beach. She's called 'Saffi' now because they had another dog called Lady, but it suits her as she's a yellow colour like saffron. She is very pretty, so I hope she finds a loving home soon.

Billy and I hope you will come and visit us in Greece before too long. Claire and Paul are always busy with building and things, so I am sure they will have a spare room for you by the summer. It is much warmer here than in England and I am writing this (with some help from Claire) sitting in the sunshine in our courtyard - and it's still only March. When I've finished we'll all go down to the beach for a run and a swim.

Life is pretty good here and the 'not so pleasant' bits of the journey are just a memory now. Sometimes we go to Paul and Claire's new house which is much bigger with lots of room to run in the garden around the trees, or just laze about under a really big pine tree. The workmen are still making it nice for us - quite major works it seems, so I don't know when we'll be able to move in. Billy and I will even have our own big room. It was a kind of garage before, but they're making it really good with a new roof just like the roof on the main house. It's just as well it is a *big* 'dog house' as we've now got a new boy, Smudge, moved in. I'll tell you more about him next time.

Bye for now,
      love   Rudi

Cautionary Tales for Drivers

Escape from Corfu Airport *by Diana Crawshaw*

We landed at Corfu airport in darkness at 4am. The airport can be quite difficult to leave if you are new to the place. After a couple of laps of the car park, we found a small road with promising arrows, but it seemed to lead to nowhere in particular.

"Let's ask someone!" I said brightly, trying to raise my boyfriend's spirits. *"Look! There's a police car! I'll go and ask them."*

The car was lurking in a side road, as if waiting to ambush somebody. I ran towards it, waving my arms in the air and smiling. This form of approach seemed to make the policemen uneasy. They turned their heads and looked the other way, reluctant to get involved with a mad woman at this stage in their operation.

"Hi!" I shouted, to make myself heard, as the 4.30 am plane from Manchester was just about to land on my head.

"Corfu Town? Which way?" I shrieked, as its wheels skimmed a nearby bush.

They turned towards me and looked at me haughtily. *"You have ... car?"* asked one, picking something out of his tooth.

"Yes, of course! It's over there!" pointing behind me without looking.

"Where? Where is car?" asked the other, suspiciously.

I looked. My finger was pointing to a blank space. Our car *pip-pipped* at me from its new position by some oil drums.

"There it is!" I said, like someone on a Blue Peter show, *"It's over there."*

"Corfu" said the helpful officer, *"is that way,"* flicking his hand (as if to swat a bluebottle) towards a clump of thorn bushes and a pile of rubbish. *"It's ... over there."*

With that he revved up and shot off into the night in the opposite direction, leaving me to try and explain how you can ask two policemen a simple question and still remain as confused as you were before ... Silly me!

Beware of Greeks Bearing Walnuts *by Diana Crawshaw*

We were staying at a remote cove in Epirus. One morning, we set off on a shopping trip to the next big village, up the steep winding road through olive groves, towards the main road at the top. As we rounded one bend, two old

women in black emerged from the trees, carrying heavy bags. They waved at us to stop. Having read that this is the customary thing to do, we stopped.

They opened the back door of the car and climbed in. *"Aghia?"* said one, tapping me on the shoulder, baring her gums. *"Neh"* I said, we could drop them off there.

We continued to climb. *"Deutz?"* said the other. *"Ochi! Inglis!"* I said, smiling to them over my shoulder. *"Inglis!"* they chorused, approvingly.

We reached the main road and they alighted, with much pushing and grunting. Then, before we could pull away, one of them reached into her bag and thrust a handful of walnuts through the window onto my lap. Her friend was doing the same through the back window, shovelling fresh walnuts onto the back seat. *"N'daxi, Efcharisto"* I yelled, thanking them as we moved off, waving.

"What lovely people." I said.

As we started down the hill towards the village, we picked up a little speed. As the road began to curve, Pete started to pump his foot up and down frantically. *"I can't slow it down!"* he yelled, "The *brakes! The brake pedal's not working!"* We were going faster. *"The ******* brakes!"*

Suddenly, he swooped forward, his hand reaching for the brake pedal.

Another loud expletive brought him back up - with two walnuts in his hand.

"Bloody walnuts! They've rolled down the floor under the pedal."

We did a lot of laughing in a hysterical manner and thanking any god who may be listening, as we cruised very gently to the nearest bar to unwind.

Moral: Never accept walnuts from a Greek yaya when driving.

Avoid Being Hit in the Pocket *by Jackie Bott*

As you'll have noticed, the 'compulsory' wearing of crash-helmets for moped/ motorbike riders has begun to take effect in Greece over the last couple of years. It's been met in Skopelos with the usual Greek attitude of 'not unless we absolutely have to', along with their own interpretation of what a crash-helmet is for. Its main purpose, from what we've seen, is to be worn over the wrist and act as a further receptacle for shopping, particularly for lady riders, who treat it as a fashion accessory or as a handbag, with all sorts of goodies spotted peeping over the rim. On no account should it be worn with the strap done up underneath the chin - the straps should be left to flap in the breeze. And, it's quite normal to see the token gesture of balancing it on the knees, ready to be popped onto the head if necessary. But the blatant disregard for all things official is the norm, with the majority of Greek riders continuing to ride hatless, and just a few visitors conforming.

It's a quirky sight to see a Greek rider, clad in their customary vest, shorts, and flip-flops, with a crash-helmet half-heartedly perched on their heads. And who can blame them, they rightly complain of them being so hot to wear. But this year things had changed. There was an abundance of riders

Safe, 'helmet free' transport

displaying helmets, in various guises and begrudgingly to boot, with quite a few of them stuck on at jaunty angles. Apparently, the new laws are more severe. The local police had a clamp-down and were issuing on-the-spot fines of €160 to anyone caught helmetless. That's a lot of money in anyone's book *(and we hear fines have gone up further since. Ed.)* It appears to have acted as a deterrent to the usual flagrant breach of the rules.

To further boost the coffers, on the day of the 'monsoon' we experienced, the police were out in force, strictly imposing the 'no parking' restrictions on the road running round the harbour. No less than 150 vehicles, illegally parked between the beginning of the harbour and the Health Centre, received tickets, bringing in some much needed revenue, along with a large dollop of resentment from locals and visitors alike. The customary 'blind eye' was not turned that day.

Holiday Wheels *by Jane Stillwell*

Anyone who has ever hired an open-top jeep or 4x4 in Greece will know that unless you happen to own a similar vehicle at home, in the unlikely event of inclement weather, putting the canvas roof back on, especially on the older models, is no mean feat.

So imagine our situation. It's the last day of the holiday; just time for last minute present buying and the final unwilling drive to the airport for the reluctant flight home. As for the hired jeep … CHAOS !! Bags everywhere, sand on the floor, empty Mythos cans quickly disposed of, making sure we hadn't left our passports or tickets in the glove box.

It is now late evening, so sadly we say goodbye and *"adio"* to our faithful holiday wheels and lovely Christos from the car hire company who comes to check we have left a full tank of petrol.

The jeep is covered in dust from the Cretan mountain roads and indeed looks very much as though we'd competed in the Acropolis rally. The canvas roof is still a crumpled heap on the floor where it has been for the duration of our holiday. Feeling rather guilty for the state of the vehicle, we apologise *"Sorry Christos ... the roof is still open and it's nearly dark."*

"OK, ok, no problem. I will put the tent back on," he replied.

Rent-a-Wreck *from Kath Riddell*

I think the ones on the bottom row are especially cheap!

Another Greek Paperchase *by Effi Hounsell*

With money in the bank, it was decided that our next priority must be to invest in a new car. Our 27 year old 800cc Suzuki jeep, a reliable and faithful comrade over the years since moving to Greece, was getting hard work for Roy to drive - especially on the National Highway to Ioanina with loads of revving TIR lorries anxious to overtake and Greek drivers, who believe it is god's will that they be first in line, overtaking recklessly. So, through November and early December, Roy trawled the car showrooms in the area for a new car that would be suitable for our needs. Smallness, by that we mean as narrow as possible, and good ground clearance being our main concerns, considering our driving terrain up here in Zagorahoria. Our good chum of many years, Apostole, suggested the Opel showroom might have something to suit. Running a car spares and lubricant shop himself he knew his business.

On 12th December 2006 Roy and a Greek speaking friend with much experience of cars visited the nearest Opel showroom, the other side of Ioanina. There was the very car for us - an Opel Aliga. Not as slender as old Suzi, but with spaces inside for everything you might want to carry - even a set of retractable step ladders would fit, should you have the need. Documents were drawn up and duly signed. A deposit of the astonishingly small sum of €100 against a car costing, together with road tax for one year, licence plates, air conditioning, everything - a BIG small car as his friend remarked - in the region of £8,000 pounds sterling. Her colour 'moonshine' (opalescent pewter I'd say) and her upholstery 'silver grey'. I'd seen it in the brochure, but only heard from Roy about its marvels. He was SO excited. Tuesday 2nd January 2007 he went to Ioanina to transfer money from his bank to the showroom's bank. Now banks here don't do that automatically. Roy had to physically draw out the full sum in cash and walk two blocks to the other bank to deposit it in the showroom's account.

Whilst he was away doing this, I took a phone call from the car showroom. They had just discovered that, the buyer being English, the number plate licensing authorities would not issue licence plates for the car until they saw Roy's Resident's Permit. We own a Greek limited company; we own our own property here; we are paid up members of the Eleniki Tourist Organisation, have a VAT number and no debts, but we can't drive the car we have paid for from the showroom until we produce a Resident's Permit. Roy has only lived in Greece for 26 years and NOW, just to take possession of our new car, we have no recourse but to take the time, effort and expense to provide an obsolete (in the light of our common EU membership) document!

Fortunately Roy was able to find his old Resident's Permit from our initial Corfu days. He telephoned the lawyer in Ioanina, took the permit, house ownership papers and a current electricity bill to him to discuss tactics. The lawyer said he must present all these papers to the local Kipi police for their stamps on a declaration to prove that he was Roy Hounsell and had lived in Koukouli for 17 years.

BUT ... the police telephoned the lawyer and it transpired that in addition he had to present a document from the Eleniki Tourist Organisation to declare we were bona fide paid up members with a licence to operate, a certificate from the Chamber of Commerce and a declaration to say we owed no Greek taxes - all this for the release of a car we had already paid for.

So, back to the lawyer and a whole day spent with him and an economist - but they were very supportive. I think they were embarrassed by the situation. After all we ARE fellow members of the European Community, or aren't we? I said it was sheer discrimination. The notary agreed - yes now a notary was involved too. Oh - The Great Greek Paper Chase never ends !

The lawyer took Roy back and forth to the Ioanina Police Office. The notary collected more requested documents and finally sent him home with instructions to present ALL accompanied by a letter of instruction from himself, to the Police in Kipi the next day. The opinion was that they, having duly stamped everything to prove Roy exists legally in Koukouli, send them to the Ioaninan Police station and the Alien Police Department then issue an up-to-date Ioaninan Resident's permit for Roy to take to the car showroom, which, incidentally, is a long drive through Ioanina and out onto the Athens road - ANOTHER whole day out of your life for car number plates! We doubted that the licence plates would be released the same day and anyway he would need to arrange for a friend to find the time to accompany him to drive the Suzuki back, or arrange an expensive taxi from Ioanina to the car showroom. Yet more days out of the Life of Roy. It seems that everything always has to be done in person. How anybody finds time to earn a living in Greece is incomprehensible.

Meanwhile I was holding the fort and manning the telephone. It must have sounded strange for incoming callers to hear me say so often *"Sorry, Roy's in Ioanina with his lawyer, economist and notary,"* and maybe next time *"Sorry, he's at the Police Station."*

Added to all that, the day Roy transferred the money to pay for the car, he had no sooner returned to hear the bad news about the permit than the phone rang again. It was the girl who handled the transaction saying that it was €1,000 short and would he drive down again to pay the difference.

Well, Roy obviously refused, but the girl said *"I cannot balance my accounts without it."* Roy was resolute and said he could not come back for several days. Shortly after she was back on the phone *"What if I drive up to Koukouli to collect the €1,000?"* So that is what she did, arriving with a couple of friends turning it into an opportunity for a 'jolly' to somewhere they had not visited before. They saw our house, the rooms, the garden and went away with the €1,000 plus €20 Roy insisted they took for petrol and the joy of not having to drive straight back to Ioanina - and of course copies of our brochure for Roy & Effi's Place. All ended happily.

That's Greece for you. Just when you feel you could punch the whole lot on the nose, they up and pull the rug from under your feet with their charming waywardness.

The following Monday Roy drove *poste haste* to deliver the permit, he had worked so hard to obtain, to the car showroom. There were more forms to fill in and sign. Very reluctantly Roy had to submit his precious Resident's Permit. The licensing department would not accept a photocopy. Then he was politely asked to see the manager in his office.

The manager carefully explained that the showroom was in the business of selling cars and while Roy was getting his paperwork together, a Greek had visited the showroom, fallen in love with the car and was ready to pay cash and drive it away then and there. There were no hold-ups with permits, so they had sold him Roy's car! The one he had paid for in full, not on the 'never never', so technically they had sold his property over his head. The manager continued in a very conciliatory way to say that an identical model had been ordered from the Athens Depot - same colour, exterior, interior, etc - but it would take another 10-15 days to arrive. They would telephone when they had it in the showroom.

Fifteen days passed and still there was no indication of when he could collect his new car. On 2nd February, a month after paying, Roy rang to ask about his car. The salesman who had transacted the sale had left the company two days earlier and Mary, who spoke English, was not on duty. The receptionist, upon hearing his name, exclaimed *"Ah yes, Mr Roy. You want to buy a car?"* "Want to? I've BOUGHT it!" The manager assured him that it was in Greek territorial waters (the car is manufactured in Poland) and would be in the showroom next week for definite, but they could not apply for licence plates until they had the car and its engine number. It would, he said, probably be available 10th to 14th February.

Mary rang us on Friday 9th February. The car was there! Exactly the same model, colour, everything - with licence plates and tax.

Roy mustered a friend to help him pick it up Tuesday 13th February. Now in Greece Tuesday 13th is superstitiously a bad day, like an English Friday 13th. Sure enough the day was a boisterous, rain-hail-and-wind day. Awful weather to drive a totally new car for the first time after 27 years in the old Suzuki Jeep. But they went ahead to collect it.

All was completed in the showroom and Roy was ready to drive his brand new car out of the showroom, a happy man. But ... no-one there could open

the great glass showroom doors to let him and the car out. Pandemonium! Finally an employee found ladders and managed to unlock the security latches at the top of the door ... and away Roy and the car went.

We've called the car 'Ollie' after a faithful friend. At last Ollie is parked in Koukouli and now Roy only has to learn what all the new buttons do.

Ed. This is a fitting update to Roy & Effi's early experiences in Greece, published as 'The Papas and the Englishman - from Corfu to Zagoria' see Reviews p165

Latest Update on Buying a Car for Greece *by Sylvia Cook*

We keep revisiting this subject and checking official rules in the light of our own desire to have a car to use when in Greece for just a few months each year. The main point seems to be that you will have to go along with whatever your local licensing office demand, which may be out of date and could differ from other regions.

We know a number of non-Greeks who have easily purchased second hand Greek registered cars with registration transferred to their name on purchase without the need to become temporary or permanent residents. This still seems the easiest route, but second hand cars are still far more expensive in Greece than in the UK.

Charges to import your existing UK car are still prohibitive in spite of Greece being taken to the European Court for not treating EU citizens fairly on this subject. Permanent emigrants can pay just 20% of the duty, which could still be more than the value of an old vehicle. Importing a new car is not so expensive, relatively - but how many people can warrant the cost of a new car, especially if it is just for part of the year at a part-time home.

Island Bus Rides *by Elaine Rowlands*

On our arrival on **Santorini** the initial view of forbidding sheer cliffs of black soon gave way to exhilaration at the steep zig-zag climb from the port as the coach made its way to **Kamari** (Καμάρι), our home for the next four days.

The next day an island tour gave us tantalizing glimpses of the main town of **Thira** or Fira (Φήρα) and **Oia** (Οία). Tricia, Len and I decided we would return by public transport the next day to spend longer in these two towns.

At the hotel reception desk we found a map of Kamari showing the only large supermarket, a Co-op, with a bus stop outside at which the bus to Thira would stop. The next morning we walked to the supermarket for 9 am, but did not know which side of the road to wait. Fortunately more knowledgeable fellow tourists soon put us right.

The bus arrived on time and quickly took us to the large bus station in Thira, which serves all the towns and villages on Santorini. It seemed that all the buses for all the destinations arrive and leave at the same time, so there was a huge scramble as locals, mostly laden with huge bags and unwieldy parcels, together with completely bemused tourists, struggled to find the right bus. A bus company official stood in the centre shouting out directions, but not really helping the confusion.

We quickly exited from the chaos and were soon exploring the narrow streets and shops of Thira town. Pausing for coffee, we watched the tenders transport people from cruise ships in the bay, before returning to the now deserted bus station to wait for our next bus, due around 12.30 pm. At this time of day most people were thinking of lunch, so the arrival of the buses was a comparatively calm affair and finding the bus to Oia was 'no problem' - as they say.

The beautiful town of Oia is a feast of the blue and white buildings so often associated with the fantastic Cycladic views seen on Greek island calendars. After a delightful lunch on a terrace overlooking the sea, we left to catch the afternoon bus back to Thira and thence to Kamari.

Four or five people sat on the steps in the shade of the supermarket. It was the middle of the afternoon and the square was almost deserted. Then the bus arrived. Suddenly we were at the back of a crowd in a struggle to get onto the bus through its two doors.

We squeezed through the middle door. Everyone seemed to have succeeded in getting aboard. I stood with bodies pressing in front of me, behind me and to the side of me. At least I had no fear of falling over as the pressure of bodies held me upright. I discovered later that Tricia was in the well of the door, terrified in case the bodies being thrown at every twist and turn of the road would cause the door to open. As for Len, I just hoped he had got on as he had disappeared from sight.

To my horror we stopped twice to pick up more passengers. I was amazed any more could fit in !

Then the conductor started to collect fares. He was not a small man, but he managed to push his way along the aisle, people standing in the tiny space between knees and the back of seats to allow him to pass.

When he reached me he dropped a few coins and we all had to get out of his way as he groped around feet, legs and bags until he found them all. It was at this point that I caught Tricia's eye and we both suddenly saw the funny side. I had to fight back mounting hysteria and was very relieved when the bus stopped to let someone out and our conductor was able to get out of the middle door and get back on the bus at the front.

In time we reached Thira safely and everyone tumbled out of the bus, including Len who had been trapped right at the back. The rest of our journey to Kamari was uneventful - but the bus ride from Oia to Thira is one I will never forget.

They Don't Make Them the Way They Used To! *by Sylvia Cook*

Cricket in a Corner of a Foreign Field *by Arthur Deeks*

If you love cricket, then visiting Greece during the season can be a time consuming, costly and emotionally painful experience. It's not just the need to seek out and purchase, daily, expensive English newspapers, to text or telephone friends and relatives for latest scores, but also the frustration from not being able to watch or play. How to combine these disparate interests?

As a post war teenager I can only remember being aware of two things about Corfu; one, that you don't sail between Corfu and Albania in case you get blown up (two British destroyers were mined in the Corfu Channel in 1946, allegedly by the Albanians); and two, the Greeks must actually play cricket, because they were short of gear and the Captain of a British warship, about to visit Corfu and wishing to help restart post war cricket on the island, made an appeal in the newspapers. Perhaps the solution to my problem would be to visit Corfu - Greek cricket's spiritual home.

Corfu town would have been the obvious choice but I was attracted to **Liapades** a village in the north west of the island just south of Paliokastritsa. It boasted a 'Cricketers Taverna' (which had hosted, amongst other English cricket luminaries, Bill Edrich and Bob Woolmer) and was close to the setting of Emma Tennant's book 'A House in Corfu' which made the area seem very attractive. The trouble with trying to kill two birds with one stone is that you invariably miss both and it probably would have been better to have stayed in Corfu town or to have hired a car. Alternatively to have gone in October (the Greeks have a long season) might have been more comfortable, because, given my aversion to hiring cars and enthusiasm for KTEL buses and add a constant temperature in the high 90's and a two kilometre walk to the nearest bus stop and you have a recipe for torpor.

In the collective sense Liapades stretches from Yefira beach, backed by the Elly Beach hotel and the Liapades Beach Hotel and Cricketers Taverna, up a very steep road for about ¾ of a kilometre past tavernas to a sort of plateau and village football pitch (where the corner is a third of the way into the tarmac road) and then up again through the charming old village to the plateia and the 17th Century church of St. Anastasia with its beautiful painted ceiling.

There are different routes up through the old village and you're sure to pass lots of old ladies who, while sitting on their steps, will direct you if you get lost. If you look exhausted enough they may invite you to sit a while - although a better grasp of Greek than mine is recommended should you be tempted to accept. However it's well worth the effort to sit outside the kafeneion in the plateia and watch the village life pass by, sipping a 'tzitzibeer' which is sold only in a few kafeneions (made without preservatives from fresh lemons and ginger, therefore often quite lively) apparently only in the summer. I know it's not exactly the high life, but if you enjoy donkeys laden with straw, the postman delivering the village post to the periptero for collection, watching the few cars that make it negotiating the handful of parking spaces and kafeneion activity, then this is for you.

If you carry on ascending through the village you can walk for miles through the most magical Midsummer-Night's Dream-like olive groves along a labyrinth of paths and tracks, with some leading down to secluded beaches like Rovinia, Limini and Liodoros.

However if it is cricket you're looking for you need to head for town, perhaps first to the offices of the Hellenic Cricket Federation in Odos Katinas Pappa 8, 49100, (very near to San Rocca Square on the road from the bus station) staffed by the very helpful and informative Elena.

The first game of cricket in Corfu was played on the 23rd April 1823 between Royal Navy officers and the local British garrison. Twelve years later Corfiots had formed two local teams allegedly called 'Little' and 'Large' - whether in terms of size or ability is unclear. In 1864, after the departure of the British, the two local clubs evolved into the 'Gongakis Company' and the 'Camvissis Club' merging in 1893 to become the Gymnastikos Club. Their sole opponents were the visiting ships of the Royal Navy which continued to feature in the progress of cricket on the island. In 1904 the Commander in Chief of the Mediterranean Fleet, with up to 40 vessels, visited the island cricket festival. In 1932 the Prince of Wales called on the island from the battleship Queen Elizabeth and, presumably expecting stronger opposition, brought with him 45 ships. After World War II, publicity by the BBC and the Daily Telegraph helped to restart the game and there were many visiting British clubs, (Lords Taverners, British Airways, Eton Ramblers, Nonnunquam - to name but a few) and the number of local teams slowly grew. Touring clubs are still warmly welcomed in Corfu and are regarded as an important aspect of the development of local cricket. Among those visiting in 2006 were Sussex 50's, Washington, and Wealdstone Corinthians CC.

The structure of cricket in Corfu gradually changed and in the 1970's it enrolled in the Greek Federation for Amateur Sport and, among other measures, promoted youth cricket with under 14 and under 18 sides encouraged in every club. In 1995 there was further development when the Hellenic Cricket Federation (HCF) was formed, becoming part of the European Cricket Council and thereby an affiliate member of the International Cricket Council.

There are now approximately 14 clubs in Greece, 11 on the island of Corfu, bearing such heroic and historical names as Gymnastikos (the oldest club) Achilleas, and Byron. Players are almost entirely of Greek extraction but a recent regulation change does allow for four year residents to play in domestic competitions. Some cricket is played in Athens (Faethon CC), Ioanina and in Thessaloniki (Nea Helvetia CC). It was clear from talking to Iosif Nikitas, the President of the HCF that the development of the game in the rest of Greece is a huge challenge requiring more than just the enthusiasm and commitment of individuals. This was exemplified by a player in a cup match that I watched between Achilleas and Gymnastikos. He lives near Ioanina and to play travels 83 kilometres on his motorbike to the closest port Igoumenitsa from where he embarks on a ferry crossing to Corfu Town - just to play cricket!

There is sadly scant coverage of cricket in the media (a situation with which minority sports in the United Kingdom would sympathise) and nothing would

help the promotion of the game more than if it became an Olympic sport, a move that would guarantee the attention of the Greek people and the media. Despite the difficulties, there is support locally from the mayor of Corfu and Nikos Georgiadis, a

Iosif Nikitas, President of the HCF

member of the Greek national parliament. In recent years a significant and growing amount of representative cricket has been played. In 2005 the 1st Kwik Cricket Primary Schools Tournament was held in Ioanina involving 120 children. HCF has also had some success in the European Indoor Championship winning in 2002 and 2005 and in the Second Division at Under 15 level in 2000.

Success in the 2005 European Affiliates Championship saw Greece finishing as Runners Up and qualifying for Division 2 of the 2006 European Cricket Council's Championships in Scotland; the first to be organised under the auspices of the International Cricket Council's World Cricket League. Division 2 consisted of France, Germany, Gibraltar, Guernsey, Greece, Israel, Jersey and Norway and after winning all three of their first round games they looked like favourites to win the tournament and promotion. Sadly it emerged that they had fielded two ineligible players and their wins were cancelled and they are now relegated to Division Four. Eligibility must be an enormous problem for countries like Greece where, for example, some of their better players may have lived or worked or even been raised abroad as part of the Greek diaspora. A related issue is that government regulations currently only allow one non EU player per team.

The Athens News in 2005 commenting on the lack of success of the HCF in spreading its appeal throughout Greece questioned *"... why hasn't it made inroads in Athens where two teams have been sputtering along without any proper facilities and where many Asian players feel so disenfranchised that they would rather have a pick-up game with their friends than get involved in the league structure?"* They also complained that the management of cricket was Corfu-centric but history is clearly against them - in England and Wales non Londoners would be familiar with that kind of attitude. I understand there is now an HCF office in Athens and a development plan for the whole of Greece in place.

On Corfu, games are mostly played on an artificial wicket on the beautiful and historic Esplanade ground in the heart of Corfu Town, with the outfield sadly slightly shrunk, due to the demands for the town's  car parking, and suffering from its use as a general open space. As a result of the proximity of the cafés on the Liston lining one side of the ground, matches on the Esplanade are sensibly played with an indoor cricket ball which does not diminish the spectacle but presumably lessens the breakages bill and the risk factor. The game I watched had a reassuringly traditional feel with lively banter among the non fielding side. It had the added dimension of waiter service as the makeshift pavilion was one of the many kafeneia lining the ground - and retsina, ouzo or even *tzitzibeer* go down very well with watching cricket. Cricket is also played at a more conventional ground near the Marina at Gouvia and a new ground is in the process of development at the Gymnastikos Club.

Cricket apart, Corfu town is surely one of the loveliest cities in Greece and well worth exploring. It is busy with visitors and years of exposure to tourism have taken their toll but that doesn't detract from its Venetian beauty (with British and French contributions). Despite foreign influences and mass tourism it is perhaps surprising that most of Corfu is still very beautiful, accessible and well worth visiting. The people remain friendly and hospitable in that traditional and very Greek way of '*filoxenia*' - despite embracing things that are quintessentially British like cricket and ginger beer.

Cricket tours can be organised for you. Look for travel companies specialising in cricket tours who advertise in cricket magazines like The Wisden Cricketer.

It's a Cats' Life by The Greek Cat Welfare Society

Everywhere you go in Greece - cities towns and villages, you will see stray cats that are thin, frightened and miserable. Only a lucky few are looked after by kind owners, or regularly fed in the wild. Dead and injured cats are often seen while newborn kittens are sometimes dumped in rubbish bins.

In cities cats live under parked cars and on derelict sites; sadly poisoning is common, although sometimes accidental, intended for rats and mice. The Greek islands are also inundated with homeless cats. Fed by kind hearted tourists during the summer months, in the winter many depend on the volunteers who leave dry food out around villages and resorts to help them fight off hunger and survive the cold. However, their breeding potential is phenomenal. An average female can produce three litters of three to four kittens annually. If the female kittens go on at the same rate the result could be over 5,000 cats from a single breeding female in four years.

In 1992 the Greek Cat Welfare Society was formed to undertake neutering of colonies of stray cats and encourage local people to have their animals neutered too. For some cats it is working. We have many Greek and international helpers dedicated to our cause, but we need more.

Fearless, Adorable Mr Woolfie by Aspasia

Early in the 90's I lost a cat of mine that I loved very much. Since then, I started feeding and caring for stray cats in my area of Athens. All these years I have seen so many terrible things and situations, that sometimes I feel I have lost the ability to laugh. But you can never say *"I stop"*. The moment you know there is a cat that needs food and treatment, you must be there. Not everyone likes stray animals in Greece, especially cats, so we must be here for them.

Every day, when it is dark, myself and many others take bags full of food and we start feeding, walking for an hour or more, 365 days of the year. Sometimes even I think I am crazy, but if you ask me why I carry on, I will tell you, it is the trust of the cats - every evening they are there waiting for me,

so I must go on.

Some of the cats I get more involved with - like Mr Woolfie.

As a little kitten he was playing fearlessly in the middle of the road near a friend's shop. She took him in and he lived in her shop, but had to be moved to the back yard when he became too active. He didn't like it alone out there and one day escaped and we could not find him. We were very sad.

About a month later he reappeared, so I took him into my home. He had grown bigger, but lost none of his fearless nature. We asked around and nearly found him a home on a farm, but on the collection day about a month later the car arrived full with 5 people, a dog and no room for Mr Woolfie.

By then I had become quite attached to this adorable little kitten, so he stayed with me. Now, almost a year old, he is still very active (most of the time). When he is full of energy he runs all over the house, slaps every other cat he meets on his route, climbs on the doors, runs up and down the stairs ... but, when he is quiet, he is the most tender, adorable cat I have ever seen. He lies next to me, touches me with his little paw, closes his eyes and he is happiness itself.

My Many Lives *by Eros*

My first memories were rather pleasant - mother's warm fur, her tender licking, and when pushing my paws against her tummy, the sweet milk filling my belly, eating, sleeping, purring ...

Suddenly there was no mummy. I was alone, crying, hungry and miserable. I was crying and running. Then a noise and a sudden terrible pain in my right foreleg. The paw was almost gone! Now on top of hunger, thirst and loneliness, I couldn't use my leg. I was desperately screaming and limping when a warm hand picked me up, making comforting noises. He gave me food. I started purring with relief.

I didn't stay long at my saviour's place. He brought me to a place where many cats live together. A lady, I call SHE, came twice a day to feed us. I was always limping behind her. SHE would pet me and put me down again. I wanted so much to stay with her and one day my wish came true. SHE took me and next I found myself in a smaller place with not quite so many other cats, but with SHE there most of the time. Bliss!

My leg didn't get better and I was taken to someone who stuck a needle into my leg. I fell asleep and woke up with one leg less! At first it bothered me, but I got used to it and can now climb trees and do anything I want to.

Each day we went together to a town in a car where we spent all day in a room with flowers and paintings, returning in the evenings to our home. One evening when SHE stopped, I thought we were home and jumped out of the slightly open window to stretch my legs. She didn't notice and drove off. What a shock! There were no trees, no friends, just strange noises. I didn't know where I was. Lost again.

I was lonely and confused, but not really starving as a kind lady, who feeds the neighbourhood strays, fed me too. I knew in my heart that SHE would find me. After many lonely days and nights I heard the familiar voice calling

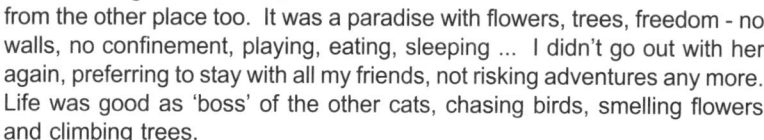

"Eros?" Oh, Lord of Cats, what joy, what a relief. It really was SHE. I lost my dignity and purring and rolling over with happiness, I was picked up and covered in kisses. Life was good, we were happy together again.

How was I found? SHE had covered nearly every shop, kiosk and post in Langada with posters about me - description, name, characteristics (three-legged). A kind person who saw me contacted her - I think the characteristic '3 legs' helped in this case.

We moved again soon after, with ALL the cats from the other place too. It was a paradise with flowers, trees, freedom - no walls, no confinement, playing, eating, sleeping ... I didn't go out with her again, preferring to stay with all my friends, not risking adventures any more. Life was good as 'boss' of the other cats, chasing birds, smelling flowers and climbing trees.

Sadly one day SHE went out in her car and did not come back. It was dreadful. We all waited and waited. Eventually SHE's friend, Sitsa, from Thessaloniki came and fed us and filled our water bowls. Another lady came and took some of my friends away in a large red van and other people came over the next few weeks. They knew my name and made a fuss of me and the others. We were looked after well, but the house was gradually being emptied and I heard them say that SHE had died. This was terrible.

Soon I was put in a horrid travelling box in the red van on a bumpy journey to a new place where I met up with all my old friends again. Some weeks later I was back in the travelling box and bumped about again. Eventually I arrived at a strange place and my box was given to a very nice lady and a little boy. I live with them now in yet another home - happy again.

Cats at a Greek sanctuary.

You can help The Greek Cat Welfare Society to help the cats of Greece and receive their regular newsletter for just £12 per year. Tel 01903 695975, see www.greekcatwelfare.moonfruit.co.uk or send subscription or a donation to The Greek Cat Welfare Society, 5 Bodmin Close, Worthing, West Sussex, BN13 3HF.

A Greek Interlude *by Judith Macbeth*

One Sunday in the late 1950's, saw the unexpected arrival on our doorstep of my dour paternal grandfather. He was in quite a distressed state, and was accompanied by a dark haired foreign lady who had apparently turned up out of the blue at my grandparents' house looking for my father. The foreigner was unfortunately unaware of the fact that my father had died some years previously. Her limited command of English, and the resulting difficulties in explaining the situation to her, proved too much for my poor grandmother. As neither grandparent was convinced the stranger had fully comprehended, despite producing photographs of my father's funeral, it was decided to bring her to meet my mother, sister and myself.

As the story unfolded, we learned that this Greek lady was a younger sister of a Greek airman who my father (an RAF officer) had met and befriended while in Greece during the war. Apparently my father had become such a regular visitor to their home, he had been treated as almost one of the family. The pieces of jigsaw were slowly fitting together. When my mother recalled the many letters containing censored news, which she had received from my father during his two and a half year absence, the characters in the story became a reality, and a bond began to form between us all.

We spent an enjoyable day with Jenny, (the simplest English equivalent of her Greek name) and, seemingly unaffected by the language barrier, she and my mother appeared to have little problem communicating.

They were both able to put faces to the people they'd each heard so much about and my mother was delighted to finally meet the person responsible for making the beautifully embroidered blouses my father had given her.

Jenny had come to England to learn the language and to marry an Englishman. Some time after this visit, news arrived of her impending wedding, with a request for me to be one of her three bridesmaids. The wedding took place in the Greek Orthodox church in Bayswater, London and the Greek guests vastly outnumbered the English.

Ted (Jenny's new husband) was a quiet pleasant man, and they eventually settled down happily to married life in Devon, subsequently with daughters Louisa and Evangelia. My mother and Jenny (by now proficient in English, if not the pronunciation) communicated regularly and we even spent a holiday with the family in Devon, where they owned a garage business.

Jenny wanted her second daughter, Evangelia, christened in Greece and suggested I may like to accompany her and the girls on the journey, staying with her relatives. Ted couldn't go, having worked hard to build up his business, he felt uneasy about leaving for any length of time.

It seemed a wonderful opportunity, so after arranging leave from my job as a hotel receptionist, we set about making plans. It was 1965 and I was approaching my 21st birthday. I had been abroad only once before, to France, but for sentimental reasons Greece had always held a fascination. I was eager and excited about the whole prospect.

Arrangements were made and it was April when Jenny and the girls came by train to London and we continued together, crossing the channel to the Hook of Holland, then on Thomas Cook's 'Wagon Lits'. The four day journey was tedious by today's standards, and would take us through Holland, Germany and Yugoslavia into Greece - the days of freely accessible air travel were yet to arrive.

A Greek sailor called Bill, joined our compartment at Rotterdam on his way home to Piraeus for a period of leave. Some time later a rather unstable looking lady of indeterminate nationality arrived, clearly in the final stages of pregnancy, and with a variety of travelling companions. Our enduring fear was that we would be called upon to act as midwives !

Once the initial inhibitions of complete strangers were overcome, things settled more comfortably. Conversation was freer with Bill as he spoke good English, although irritatingly he and Jenny frequently lapsed into Greek. My suspicions were subsequently confirmed when he later asked to meet me in Athens. Throughout the journey he had been subtly investigating my status with my chaperone, before finally venturing his formal request to meet me. Such strange customs were new and alien to me.

As we reached the Greek border a wave of jubilation coursed through the train, as it jerked unsteadily to a halt. Doors opened and people jumped out, undeterred by the steep drop to the parched earth beneath. There were spontaneous whoops of delight as everyone embraced in wild abandon. Much later at Athens, a sea of strange olive skinned faces met us as we pulled into the station. Although it was dark, the lights threw out a sickly yellow glow, and feeling utterly exhausted and dirty, I was already homesick and wished I could collapse into my own bed to sleep for a week. After the luxury of my first night's proper sleep for four days, my perspective greatly improved and I felt better disposed towards our sojourn in Kypseli, Athens where Jenny's sister lived.

Marina was a short rotund, homely lady, with a disconcerting habit of snorting, which she did regularly. Her husband, Thomas, was tall and thin, with pointed features. As a pair they were reminiscent of Jack Sprat and his wife. Thomas had huge prominent eyes and thick bushy eyebrows which met in profusion on the bridge of his long narrow nose, giving him a curiously gaunt and ferocious expression. This unfortunately belied the gentler nature carefully concealed beneath. He was a man of few words.

Of their two sons, Evangelos, the younger appeared the least amenable. His short overweight physique lay testament to the vast amounts of chips he devoured. His argumentative nature seemed appropriate for the political profession he hoped to follow.

Gregory, however was refreshingly different, and the only member of the family able or eager to speak English. This, together with his quiet friendly manner soon made him my ally and confidant.

Keen to improve his already adequate command of English, he used every opportunity to talk to me - endlessly. He spent time showing me places of interest - apart from the Acropolis and its nearby flea markets he took me to the top of Mt. Lykabettos, showed me parks, student nightclubs with wonderful live traditional Greek music which I loved, cafes and restaurants. In one restaurant in Tourkolimano, I learned it was best not to feed stray cats. I had instinctively responded with a titbit to a persistent pawing at my leg, whereupon we were surrounded by a plethora of ravenous marauding cats. We were rescued by the deft aim of an unscrupulous waiter. To his credit Gregory listened sympathetically to my animal lover's feelings of concern regarding this incident, providing yet more fuel for our discussions. We talked at length of the differences in our ways of life, and doing so platonically was refreshing and a relief. He explained how he passionately wanted to be a doctor, which he knew would involve many years of study.

In stark comparison, although two years older, I felt uncertain about my future, at odds with so much of myself and emotionally confused.

Gregory asked many questions, not least about boyfriends, and seemed intrigued with my current situation. I explained how five months previously I had met and fallen hopelessly in love with someone from a different culture, living on the other side of the world. Since he returned home, we wrote constantly. Our next meeting was due shortly after my return when his work would bring him briefly back to London, with whatever ensuing consequences.

Meanwhile, shortly before my departure for Greece, I had complicated my life further by striking up a friendship with Roberto, a handsome persua-

sive Italian, who worked at the same hotel. He had asked for my holiday address, and by now, the daily letters arriving from both suitors only confused me further. They also aroused some interest from my Greek hosts, who were already trying their hands at matchmaking, although quite with whom I wasn't sure !

Gregory thought the whole matter vaguely amusing, but remained apparently unconcerned and aloof from these idle family prognostications. Later however, having rather unwillingly contrived to help me set up a liaison with sailor Bill from the train, and hearing my confession of an unscathed escape from Bill's dishonourable intent, Gregory displayed uncharacteristic irritation at my apparent stupidity.

There were numerous relatives and friends of Jenny's to meet, but nonetheless I was relieved when it was time to go to Jenny's elderly parents on the island of Poros, where Evangelia's christening would take place.

Jenny, the two girls and myself departed for the tiny island of Poros in the Saronic Gulf south of Athens, a sea journey of some four hours from Piraeus. I was immediately captivated by this small tranquil picturesque island, with its wonderful smells of pine and lemons, and felt instinctively content in its balmy ambience.

Jenny's parents' house, was situated at the bottom of a hillside overlooking the sea, and I felt highly honoured to have been assigned the room with a balcony overlooking such an incredible view. I could hardly wait to write home about it. Her parents were obviously delighted to see her and Louisa, and to meet their youngest granddaughter for the first time. Evangelia was, like myself in contrast to all the locals, blonde haired. As a result, we attracted attention wherever we went. At first it was fun, but after a while the novelty wore off and it became tiresome and ultimately embarrassing.

Jenny's father was the village priest, and as such a highly revered member of the community. He had a full snow white beard reaching to his waist and equally long white hair, which he wore tied back in the customary little knot behind his head, on top of which sat his tall black hat. Beneath thick white eyebrows, his piercing dark brown eyes fixed a stern but kindly gaze from a suntanned face. His noble presence automatically dominated any room he entered and any company he joined. Whenever he walked down the street, children would call *"Papou!"* and run up to kiss his hand, eager to receive his approving pat.

Yaya, Jenny's mother, clearly showed the strains of frequent childbearing. Her small rounded frame now bent and weary with age, her brown wrinkled face, twinkling eyes and uneven smile bore evidence perhaps of an earlier stroke. However, her kindly acknowledging nods and gentle muses were reassuring, and when occasion demanded, she could still raise her voice sufficiently to demand instant response. Neither of Jenny's parents spoke nor understood any English, but again, this presented no barriers.

The time until Gregory's arrival was spent with the two children and myself getting to know their many cousins. Due to the lack of any common spoken language, our communication was based on patience and understanding at simple levels. Each benefiting from this new experience, we easily became friends. Those who spoke even a modicum of English always seemed eager to put their scant knowledge to the test.

One of Jenny's sisters-in-law and her children occupied the ground floor of their grandparents' house, a temporary arrangement until they were able to join their father who had emigrated to Australia. This was the brother who had befriended my father many years before, whom I would not therefore meet.

Without Gregory's trusted companionship, I soon recognised how stifling an unchaperoned existence could be. There had been an inquisition when I briefly met a group of Americans while out with the girls. These lads had suggested taking me for a drink at the local café. Later that day, when two of them called at the house, they were politely but firmly sent on their way.

Visit to George's farm

In stark contrast, when we were invited to visit the farm of a pilot friend of the family, who happened to be a quite handsome and eligible bachelor, named George, the attempts at throwing us together were hardly subtle. I therefore felt greatly relieved when Gregory briefly arrived from Athens, for the culmination of the religious festivities at Easter which coincided with our visit.

Although he had to return immediately afterwards and would miss the christening, I realised the strength of his friendship and how unintentionally I had come to rely on him, if only to avoid the justification of every sortie I made.

On Good Friday night we watched the candlelit procession, carrying the symbolic coffin of Christ, winding down the hillside to the square, where, it seemed the whole island had gathered. The next night we were back at the church again, culminating with the jubilation at midnight and cries of *"Christos anesti"* (Christ is risen) and then feasting well into the early hours. During the days prior to this there had been a traditional fasting of certain foods including meat. While other members of the household dutifully spent hours in church, Gregory and I had been able to secretly prepare and eat the forbidden foods. It was quite a relief to end the fast and eat relatively normally.

Dawn broke on the day of the christening. The family was up early and assembled on the quay ready to board the waiting flotilla which took us up the stretch of water on the first leg of our journey, to the church where the ceremony would take place. Several icons accompanied us on the voyage; each carefully covered in spotless crisp white wraps. Each time we passed a church or chapel, those in charge of these prized possessions blessed themselves and kissed the icons. After a sea journey of some thirty minutes, we alighted onto the narrow jetty, where a train of rather thin lethargic donkeys patiently waited to take the more infirm members of the party up the steep narrow winding track to the church; a tiny deserted whitewashed building at the top of a hill surrounded by lemon groves.

A distinctly stale and musty odour assailed us as the low wooden door was opened for us to enter, but soon the little church was filled to capacity. The ceremony consisted of seemingly endless monotoned readings, interspersed with regular blessings, all delivered by Jenny's father, whose bespectacled appearance made him look even more austere than usual. The renditions complete, the baptism took place and poor naked Evangelia was briefly submerged in a huge metal vessel, her lovely blonde hair and body anointed thoroughly with oil. Despite this ordeal, surrounded by all this unfamiliarity,

the child remained thankfully unperturbed as she was dried and re-clothed.

Afterwards the party set off again to Kardassi, higher still up into the lemon groves, to a restaurant with a raised eating area and long tables placed end to end, completely canopied by grape vines, providing both shade and a welcome breeze. By now, the sun was very hot.

The scene it overlooked was a breathtaking panorama of steep multicoloured green hillsides flanked by lemon and olive trees descending sharply to the brilliant blue sea some distance below. We sat down to a glorious traditionally seasonal feast of a whole lamb roasted on a spit with rosemary and other herbs, the like of which I had never seen nor tasted before. The whole experience was one I will never forget. As I gazed on, dreamily savouring this magical scene, I experienced a reluctance at the prospect of going home, but I knew I had no choice.

Jenny and the girls would stay on in Athens longer than planned, so I would have to travel home alone. I decided to return by air, and it was here that George, the pilot friend, turned up trumps and arranged my flight from Athens. The next day, Jenny, the girls and myself were up at 6 am, to say our goodbyes on leaving Poros, arriving in Piraeus to be met by Gregory.

That evening as Gregory and I sat in the Dionysos café overlooking the floodlit Acropolis which dominates the city, enjoying the balmy warmth of Athens by night, we reflected on all that had transpired in the short month since our first meeting. My stomach churned when he looked at me with his warm unflinching hazel eyes and asked if I had resolved any of the problems I'd brought with me. I half smiled. We both knew he needed no reply. We continued chatting in what had become our easy custom, promising to write. Gregory was planning a visit to London the following year and I hoped he would have time to stay at least a few days with us.

Gregory managed a short stay with us the following year, by which time his plans to become a doctor were well under way. It was some years later while Jenny was staying with my mother, that we all met up again, and I introduced Gregory to my husband and two sons.

Gregory, now a consultant and happily married with a daughter, had stopped by briefly while in London on business, although physically fuller in stature, his calm gentleness remained unchanged. During that short meeting, we recalled our endless discussions, and how we ate the forbidden food during the religious fast all those years ago. I reminded him of how he'd been my ally.

He looked at me with those warm familiar hazel eyes and smiled as he said *"You make it sound as if we had a past, but we haven't."*

Greece in England *by Peter Greaves*

In the cultural wilderness of rural Derbyshire I look for any opportunity to support the spread of Greek civilisation. I recently had two contrasting opportunities.

The PTA decided on a Greek themed evening as a fund raiser. The village hall was duly decked with trailing vines and taverna style tables with candles and flowers. The village ladies, under Brenda my wife's guidance, produced very acceptable and palatable Greek dishes, (I dealt with the telephone call from the supermarket enquiring which shelf the big beans were on). I provided CDs of Greek music from my collection and a set of questions to educate the masses in Greek achievements in sport, history, myths, films, etc for a Quiz. The evening was sell out - 55 tickets and a waiting list.

Now, it may have been partly my fault but everyone seemed determined to enjoy themselves and I thought it only sociable to share some of that raki that we had been keeping since receiving it as a parting gift a couple of years ago. Raki doesn't seem to have a sell or use by date. To be strictly accurate I was too frightened to drink it all myself, but it certainly added to the jollity of the evening. Shortly after the raki drinking I lost control of the question and answer session.

Next day everyone said what a good time they had had, but my recollection was that it was more Club 18-30 in Faliraki than a cultural event. Still we raised £700 for the PTA.

(If you want to test your own knowledge, or hold a Greek Quiz Night, you may wish to use some or all of the questions opposite, adapted from those we posed at our PTA event. Answers on page 174.)

In contrast on a wild, wet, and windy winter's evening we headed up into the hills for an event sponsored by 'Live and Local' who aim to bring artists of all kinds to rural communities. In this case it was the 'Plastic Chairs'. Again the reading room of this village hall was arranged taverna style with Greek food, but with a full range of family ages present. The group were excellent, producing authentic Greek music with bouzouki, guitar and vocals. Their unusual name, *Plastikes Karekles*, suits their malleable group format which can be 3, 4, 5 or 6 performers drawn from a pool of musicians. You can find out more about them on www.theplasticchairs.com. They play regular Friday nights in Yialousa restaurant near Russell Square in London. Apart from playing, they took time to educate their audience, explaining what their music was about and they encouraged audience participation in dancing.

Leaving there and playing their CD 'Bouzoukology' on the way home was a much more 'grown-up' Greek experience.

Greek Quiz Questions

Sport

1. What year were the first Olympics?
2. What event(s) were in the first Olympics?
3. Which year were the first Olympics of the modern era?
4. Over what distance is the marathon run?

Films

1. 'Zorba the Greek' was based on a local character near which Greek resort?
2. Where was the setting and filming for 'Captain Corelli's Mandolin'?
3. On which Greek island was much of 'Shirley Valentine' filmed?
4. On which island was the exterior filming for Guns of Navorone?

Geography

1. Does London have more, less, or the same average rainfall as Corfu?
2. What is the highest mountain in Greece?
3. How many permanently inhabited islands are there in Greece? (to 10)
4. Where is the Monks' Republic?
5. Which part of Greece was the last to be be annexed in 1947/8?
6. Which city do Greeks call The Polis?

History

1. What happened on Santorini around 1450BC?
2. Where did the famous 300 Spartans fight?
3. Which Queen watched the battle of Actium from the Greek coast?
4. Which part of Greece was a British Protectorate 1815-1864?
5. When did the Greek War of Independence start?
6. Which British poet died in support of the Greek War of Independence?
7. Which British poet was buried on Skyros in 1915?
8. Which WWII battle was fought off the most southerly point of mainland Greece?

Mythology

1. Who sought the Golden Fleece?
2. Who laboured through Twelve Tasks?
3. Who worked the loom waiting for her husband to return to Ithaca?
4. Who led the archaeological excavation at Mycenae?
5. Where, in ancient times, was known as the 'navel of the world'?

General

1. What is ouzo made from?
2. Where was Prince Philip the Duke of Edinburgh born?
3. What is the Greek National holiday on 28th October called?
4. What is the name of Athens' airport, opened in 2001? *(answers p174)*

Travel Notes

Captured by Maria *by John Cook*

A few years ago my wife and I made our first trip to Crete, staying in the picturesque resort of **Elounda** (Ελούντα) in the north east. As we had just enjoyed the trials and tribulations of our daughter getting married, all we wanted to do was crash out and relax for a couple of weeks. We didn't hire a car or go any further than the resort of **Agios Nikolaos** (Αγ. Νικόλαος) a little further along the coast.

It was not until the last couple of days that we realised there were some very non-touristy villages just behind Elounda, one of which was **Pano** (or Epano) **Elounda** (Επάνω Ελούντα meaning 'upper Elounda') which, apart from having the local cemetery, has spectacular views over the coast, Elounda and the surrounding countryside.

I had ventured there early one morning towards the end of our holiday and on the following evening persuaded my wife that we should head in this direction for an evening stroll prior to returning to eat in Elounda. I had noticed on my previous reconnaissance that there was a small bar at the lower end of the village and thought we may call in for a drink on the way back.

As we approached the village, passing scruffy little dwellings with a few chickens, goats and other animals wandering around rocky unkempt surroundings, we came to a junction which lead straight up to the cemetery. Rather than going straight to the village we took this turning to take a closer look and spent a while enjoying the serenity of what was a beautiful place to be laid to rest. It was so quiet and peaceful. We shared our time there with locals who were bringing fresh flowers or just visiting relatives' graves. *Kalisperas* were exchanged in whispers, as if to raise ones voice would have disturbed the inhabitants; but somehow it just seemed right to behave in this way.

When eventually we had drunk in the view enough to have almost made ourselves giddy, we exited to find that we were now at the top end of the village. The village had been built on a large rocky outcrop and had only dirt or concrete footpaths and, so far as we could see, no access for vehicles, nor could we tell how old the place was. It was clearly older than the only date we saw, on the little white church right in the middle of the settlement, built as recently as the 1930's.

Re-entering the village through a little pathway, we had not gone more than 20 metres or so when we were seized upon by an elderly (ie older than us) lady in a flowery dress, who, without any obvious effort or persuasion, got us to sit in her little courtyard (a very grand expression for what it was), but only after dispatching the younger of two other ladies who had been sitting there chatting with our host. We were left with our captor, who we soon discovered was Maria, and her even more elderly sister.

Other than the pleasantries, we have no Greek vocabulary and it soon became clear that Maria and her sister spoke no English either. Their home didn't give us any clues as to why we were stopped there, but having visited Greece for many years and with the state of calm brought on by the cemetery, we didn't really mind being there.

After we had exchanged greetings with Maria, given our names and assurances that we were not German, but 'Anglika' (although we are from Wales), she asked us whether we wanted beer or lemonade (two words of her non-Greek vocabulary). We opted for beer and off went Maria into the building leaving us with her sister as temporary, smiling, but not speaking, company. She returned with two large bottles of cold Amstel, glasses and a plate of grapes.

At this point we noticed the small stained glass window above the door of her residence and it dawned on us that this may in fact be licensed premises of some sort. Off went Maria again to quickly return with another plate of sliced tomatoes and olives. By now we had managed to tell her about our children and grandchildren and she had conveyed by sign language and the word 'caput' that both hers and her sister's husbands were resting in the place we had latterly come from. Anyway Maria disappeared for a longer period and as we exchanged further smiles with her sister we could hear

what sounded like cooking noises coming from within. Sure enough Maria returned with two bowls of what looked like porridge, but was in fact a slightly salty but nonetheless tasty rice pudding.

With time getting on and us thinking we should not outstay our welcome, we asked Maria how much we owed her. She soon produced a little bit of paper with the cost of the beers, to which we added a reasonably generous tip to allow for the little meze she had pre- pared for us. At this point we took our leave, but not before Maria insisted on giving us a large bag of grapes and saw us on our way down through the middle of the village.

By now many people were sat outside their homes. As we made our way we were greeted with a succession of *"kalispera, kalispera"* until eventually we reached the little bar we had originally intended to visit. As we got closer we recognised the younger lady who had been sent out by Maria to make room for us, sitting outside with what must have been nearly half the village population.

We were once again greeted by a cacophony of *kalispera*s, but decided on this occasion to keep walking, as otherwise we may have ended up there all evening. One thing that did occur to us - perhaps from their knowing smiles or the slightly heightened ring to their *kalispera*s - we felt sure that they all knew we had spent time with Maria.

It was with a considerable feeling of well-being that we left the village, a bit as if we were walking on air. As we approached the more touristy aspects of Elounda, we reflected that this sort of encounter is what makes Greece such a magical place to visit.

The next morning we shared details of our experiences the previous evening with a family staying at our apartments and were surprised when they re- acted with peals of laughter. It transpired that they too had been 'captured' by Maria several years earlier and not only had they revisited her on their subsequent holiday, but were planning a further return trip that very evening. Apparently their daughter had wanted to visit the toilet on the first occasion and was somewhat put off by the crude facilities available - just a bucket at that time. However on their second visit Maria had obviously had some improvements made as she proudly announced to them that she now had a proper toilet.

Brief Encounters on Ithaca *by Arthur Deeks*

It really wasn't quite as I remembered it but then few things ever are and I had been away 2½ times longer than Odysseus. The Cave of the Nymphs,

for example, where on his return Odysseus was supposed to have stashed his prezzies from the Phaeacians, was so much smaller and scruffier. I also didn't remember all those bits of stalactites or 'mites stuck all over the place outside. Last time I was there our beloved retired headmaster leader made us all go in with flaming torches and read bits of Homer. It also had a sad disused ticket office (as did the Palace of Alalkomenes which at the end of the day is only a bit of cyclopean wall) as if the circus had moved on. Perhaps the recent challenging by scholars of the historical location of Odysseus' legendary homeland had caused some uncertainty. It's a bit like saying Robin Hood didn't come from Nottingham - which of course he didn't !

Of course Ithaca is essentially as captivating as it ever was and in early May is particularly beautiful, green and with wild flowers in abundance, albeit a tad chilly in the evenings. For Harry and me it became the island of brief, but always interesting, encounters and conversations. It also seems to be the place for the purposeful British as they walk, sail, paint, study wild flowers or butterflies and antiquities. As the island is relatively small and it's early season, you keep bumping into the same people and receiving progress reports - like the lepidopterist couple who identified increasing numbers of butterflies finally reaching, to them, a disappointing 32.

Even arriving in the small hours of the morning didn't detract from the pleasure in seeing **Vathi** (Βαθύ) again and finding our superior and spacious accommodation. *"Look Harry, a shower cubicle!"* I pulled the sliding door and the runner came away and clanged on the floor and I sashayed across the bathroom clutching a large panel. Harry gave me his Oliver Hardy 'here's another fine mess you've gotten me into' look before he worked out how to restore it (together with the detached shower head and the toilet ejector

seat - Martin-Baker eat your heart out). I know Harry's Greek plumbing skills are admirable, but for goodness sake, what other visitor to Greece packs a roll of plumber's tape in his suitcase.

The trouble with writing articles, and guide books I guess, is that by the time they are published some things have altered. There are, of course, seasonal changes, recommended tavernas are boarded up or full of cobwebs, prices vary and bus timetables change. The latter was the first obstacle we encountered and, being chronologically challenged, transport is pretty important to us. Now Harry and I are a bit averse to hiring cars, preferring the freedom of (if not sometimes slightly mythological) KTEL buses. We were assured that there was one bus a day from Vathi, at 11 am, and it would get us to the north of the island, which would suit us just fine. The experience was like taking part in Waiting for Godot (with apologies to Samuel Beckett). Scene: a road by the harbour at Vathi - a bus stop - morning. Two English tourists studying a small notice on the bus stop are joined by two more and engage in desultory conversation.

"Can't do anything about it."

"It hasn't come yet then."

"It says here 'Apo 10.30'."

"The rep definitely said 11."

Two more tourists arrive. *"Not come yet then. She said 11?"*

"Yes, she definitely said 11."

Two more people arrive. *"No bus? It's almost 11."*

"It says 'Apo 10.30' on the sign."

"She definitely said 11." More tourists arrive, reaching unlawful assembly proportions, or as Harry helpfully observed, enough for a cricket team, and suggested I go and check.

I asked in the card shop. They thought it only went in the high season and referred me to the travel agency. They were not sure and suggested that I try the pharmacy

Adapted from Efstathiadis Road Atlas

opposite the bus stop. The pharmacist said he would go and ask in the souvenir shop next door, returning to say that she thought it went very early for the schoolchildren. I reported back to the crowd which sighed collectively and dispersed. Others later reported that they had made it their mission to seek out the bus driver who had confirmed that it probably went at 6 - unless he went at 5.30 am.

The issue then was, given that we could probably do a fair bit of the south of the island on foot, how to cover the rest which was beyond our capabilities without mechanical assistance. There were no 'Scuter's for Rend' anymore and so we broke with the habits of a lifetime and decided to hire a car. I drove because Harry is a graduate of the Toad School of Motoring with a shallow knowledge of the finer points of cars - he thinks the Kyoto Accord is a Japanese car and a rev counter an instrument for counting passing clergymen.

And so, armed with a copy of Sylvia and Terry Cook's 2001 Greek-o-File article, we set off around the island on pretty well deserted roads and soon found ourselves in **Stavros** (Σταυρός). After fortifying ourselves with a portion of the unique local delicacy 'Rovani' (honey & rice cakes) from Margaritas café, we visited the tiny archaeological museum as perfectly described in the Cooks' article. To our surprise, as it was a bit out of the way and there were no parked vehicles, it was packed to the gunwales with artists, mainly female, seated on small stools, all earnestly drawing the artefacts on display. Harry and I were turning away when the delightful Greek-Australian curator insisted we squeezed in as she was just about to address the group. So feeling as though we had crashed a private party we flattened ourselves against the wall. At the end of her fascinating and knowledgeable talk I was trapped against a case of bronze bits by a very severe looking artist who regarded me over her spectacles with the sort of expression that took me back well over half a century to the headmistress of St Mary's Infants School.

"What, is that?", she hissed indicating an amorphous lump of bronze.

I stared at it with her, wishing I had paid more attention to the talk and looking for a way out through the massed ranks of artists before I got detention or lines.

"Well, what did she say it was?"

I peered at it intently hoping for inspiration, and stared at it again. My mind a blank, I shuffled awkwardly, *"I dunno - er, a nymph perhaps."*

She sighed and, seeing a gap open in the ranks of artists, I scuttled to the door. My exit was blocked by the custodian who indicated the visitors' book. Why is it that I can never think of anything witty, apposite or any unused superlatives when faced with these books? However brownie points were soon earned when I offered the custodian my crumpled copy of the article

from Greek-o-File that mentioned her and the museum. She received it with both hands and with genuine delight as though it were some delicate historical artefact - which I suppose it is.

We pressed on to **Frikes** (Φρίκες), a pretty little village harbour where we studied the marble tablet, set in the hillside, which commemorates the taking of a German vessel by local resistance fighters during the Second World War. We moved on to **Kioni** (Κιόνι), another picturesque village and harbour where our interest in the war memorial provoked a local to expound in great detail the wartime history of Frikes and Kioni and indeed the whole of Ithaca, all in impeccable English. This encouraged us to enquire if he happened to know the score in the Test Match. He didn't, but he knew a man who did and referred us to 'Vanilla' whom he said was a cricket fanatic and lived in a lovely stone house by the quayside, where we sat and watched the flotilla yachts come and go while plucking up courage.

Despite my reluctance and some trepidation, Harry finally knocked on his door and was greeted by the charming and friendly Costas Raftopoulos (although he is perfectly happy with his nickname) with whom we talked cricket and rugby for the next hour, including his experiences with many first class South African players. We agreed that both Frikes and Kioni are excellent for just 'chillin'.

It is an island with walks to suit pretty well everybody (including, the guided variety available locally

Harry and 'Vanilla'

with Island Walks and Creative Ithaki) and a fair sprinkling of beaches some with cantinas or small tavernas. Our favourite was **Dexa** (in a delightful olive grove with the Georgios Snack Bar) and **Loutsa** with its small Venetian fort and cannons guarding the entrance to Vathi.

One of our early brief encounters was on the way to the Cave of the Nymphs when we were pursued by Steve, a kindly Englishman semi expatriate, with a huge bottle of water when he learned we had forgotten to take any with us. Later he and his wife regaled us with stories of the local eccentric, a man you would not want as your neighbour, while we drank tea and cold beer on his veranda.

Whether by foot, car or bus (if you ever find it) what is inevitable is that you will encounter large wind sculptured rocks and stunning views either over the **Gulf of Molos**, or across to Kefalonia, or to Astakos and beyond on the mainland, particularly from the scenic roads to and from Stavros. If however you are of a claustrophobic nature and wish to escape the island or feel you must go down to the sea again there is always the daily (except Saturday) ferry to Patras leaving at 7 am.

Rainy day options, apart from the Museum at Stavros, include the small archaeological museum in Vathi and the nautical and folklore museum which contains some interesting shipping memorabilia. Our final enjoyable yet humbling encounter was at Dexia Beach where we met a veteran of the

Kings Royal Rifle Corps who was awarded a Military Medal during the WWII campaign in North Africa.

Byron got it about right when he said *"if this island belonged to me I would bury all my books here and never go away."*

Bearing in mind the caveats earlier in the article regarding seasons, we found the following worth a visit:

Kafeneia:

Probably the most impressive, although hardly a kafeneion, is the very stylish *café bar* located in the impressive converted neoclassical mansion of shipowner G. Drakoulis on the sea front.

The Odysseus in the square, next to the souvenir shop, is very pleasant, reasonable and well positioned although the more traditional one with uncomfortable chairs and unsmiling staff one street back on Odos Doureiou is much cheaper.

Tavernas:

In the same road is the *To Trehantiri* which has a certain back street charm but don't bother to ask ex sailor Gerry (Gerazimos Dorizas) for a menu as it bears no relation to what's on offer. The inside offers a rare example of an egg box ceiling, the sort of thing which was the height of trendy style in British youth clubs in the 50's, however the food is good and very cheap.

O Niko just back from the front serves complimentary pre-orektika slices of delicious fried stuff and the rest of the traditional food is very good. Opposite is the *Kalkanis* which apparently stays open all year round and is also excellent and cosy for early season evenings. *To Kohili* on the waterfront finally opened, just before we left, and was worth waiting for the wonderful lamb and feta cheese in paper parcels.

How to get to Ithaca

By Air - Scheduled flights via Athens to Kefalonia, or charter direct to Kefalonia

By Ferry - from Kefalonia - Ag. Efimia, Fiscardo, Sami; Lefkada - Vassiliki, Nidri; Mainland - Astakos, Patra.

Package Tour Operators - Best of Greece, CV Travel, Greek Islands Club, Inn Travel (walking), Ionian Island Holidays, Island Wandering, Kosmar, Olympic Holidays, Oneira Holidays, Seafarer, Simpson Travel, Sunsail, Sunvil

Profile of Lipsi *by Mary Lambell*

Lipsi (Λειψοί) is one of the smaller islands of the Dodecanese, with Leros to the south and Patmos to the north west.

For such a small island Lipsi is surprisingly well connected by boats of various kinds. Its amenities are good too: schools for all ages including a fine nursery school, a resident doctor and two dentists. There are about 650 permanent inhabitants, many more having emigrated to America and Australia, particularly Hobart, Tasmania, though many return in the summer.

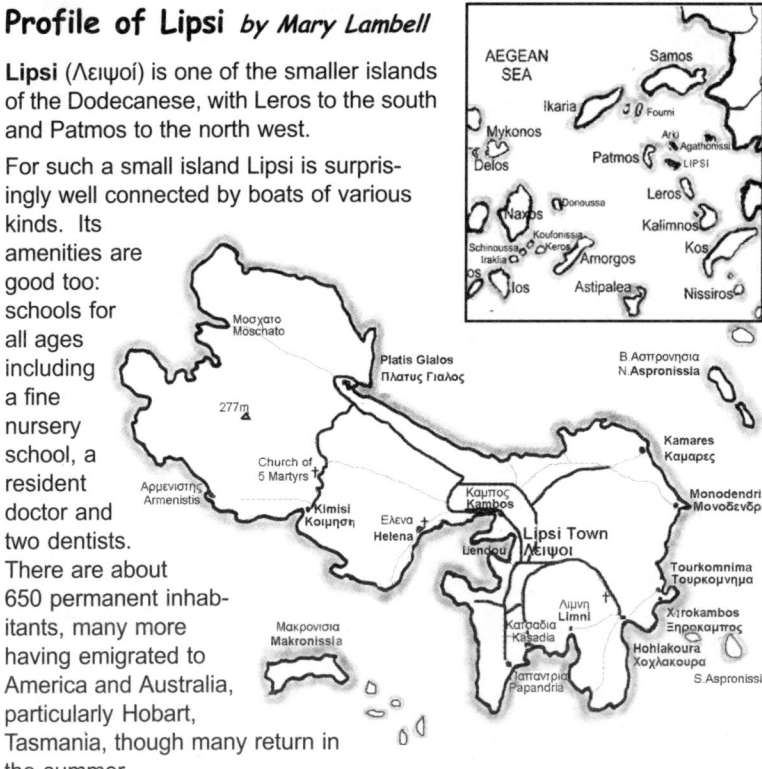

There is just one settlement, based round the attractive and well maintained harbour, with fishing boats and fishermen mending their nets on the quayside. It is also a popular stopping place for sailing boats.

Lipsi background

☐ *According to local legend Lipsi was Calypso's island in the Odyssey.*

☐ *Not much in the way of records exist from ancient times, but the first inhabitants were Carians from Asia Minor, followed by Dorians from the north of Greece.*

☐ *Some pottery has been found from the Mycenaean and Geometric periods (about 1400 to 800BC)*

☐ *In 730AD as part of the Byzantine Empire Lipsi was of strategic importance; it was badly affected by Byzantine/Arab conflicts.*

☐ *In 1088 Lipsi, with Arki and Patmos was handed over to Osios*

Christodoulos by the Byzantine Emperor Alexis Komninos. This led to the building of the Monastery on Patmos. Lipsi remained linked to Patmos for 556 years, the land being used for grazing and farming. Several monasteries and hermitages were founded (eg Kimissi and Panaghia tou Harou).

❑ When the Turks invaded Greece in 1523 Lipsi was not occupied but made to pay taxes and was subjected to some raids. Many Greeks abandoned the island at this time.

❑ In 1669 Lios, fleeing from the Turks in Crete, founded the populated area of today, having first lived in a cave above Liendou Beach. His house was the first in today's Lipsi town.

❑ 1821 Lipsi played an important part in the War of Independence, sheltering rebels. It managed to remain independent for some years but in 1932 became part of the Dodecanese under Italy. The islanders determined to show their allegiance to Greece: hence the predominance of blue and white houses and churches.

❑ In 1947 Lipsi was reunited with Greece at the same time as the other Dodecanese.

Languid, Low-key Lipsi *by Mary Lambell*

'The island is 16 square metres', according to the only map we found available on the island. **Lipsi** is indeed small, but not that small - 16 square kilometres according to the Greek version. The same map contains other Delphic translations, like *"Why the nights are full moon lit, are like a lie, like a dream. Without face-control, bright signs plainly without show-offs, freely as each one feels, can stay up until the early hours....."* I looked at the Greek version to see what they translated as 'face-control', but they used the English, even in the German and Italian translations! What on earth does it mean? Basically I believe it is saying that there are no neon lit or gaudy signs, and that night life is traditional and low-key.

To reach the island we flew to Kos, and enjoyed a pleasant few hours in Kos town before boarding the Flying Dolphin for a 2-hour journey to Lipsi via Kalymnos and Leros. The return journey was by the catamaran, Dodecanese Express, more comfortable and with the same journey time.

Our arrival (in May 2006) coincided with the annual visit of a group of specialist doctors (known as Ομάδα Αιγαίου) who go round the various islands offering their expertise to the inhabitants. They were greeted by the town band and with great festivity. We learnt that they had financed the very fine children's playground, and a new medical centre to be built. Their presence was particularly fortunate for one holidaymaker who fell whilst out jogging and cut her ear badly on a piece of wire fencing *(coincidentally this was another Greek-o-File reader Chris Duckworth, see 'Good Timing for a Bad Trip' p14).*

I tested the dental facilities on the first day of our holiday when a temporary filling dropped out. An appointment was swiftly made. I was assured that only a small part of the filling was lost and told to return if there were any further problems. In neither of these cases was any charge made nor any insurance document requested.

The island has several of the usual Greek small super-markets selling everything you need and more; also two bakeries, a traditional one still using a wood-fired oven, and the 'new bakery' also serving as

the *zacharoplasteio* with a wonderful assortment of cakes and ice creams. Lipsi bread is particularly good we thought, and brown was on offer too. There was no ATM machine when we were there but a smart new bank with machine was being prepared and due to open on June 1. There are two hairdressing salons, a fish shop, pharmacy and post office, also a small museum, but it rarely opens. We never made it.

Eating and drinking requirements are more than catered for, with a number of tavernas, some of which were still in the process of opening up in May. Kalypso (Καλύψω) prided itself on its organic vegetables. Yannis was busy extending his eponymous taverna, painting chairs and tables blue, and only opened on our last evening, by which time we had our favourite, To Pefko (Το Πεύκο), where a very friendly Nikos had an excellent menu - Greek food with flair in beautiful surroundings. Most eating places are around the harbour, but there are some up in the older part of the town. Lipsi boasts three traditional ouzeries, popular with locals and visitors alike. Sophocles' ouzerie specialised in grilled octopus meze.

Because the island is small it is possible to walk everywhere. There is no car hire, but there are mopeds, 2 taxis and a minibus service to some of the beaches in high season. Many of the walks are on roads which are increasingly replacing tracks, but they are quiet. There are beaches all round the

island, no sunbeds nor umbrellas, the only shade being trees on some of them. The nearest beach to Lipsi town is **Liendou,** (Λιεντού), sandy with shade from tamarisk trees. The sea is shallow for a long way out, so ideal for children. Next round the bay is **Kambos** (Κάμπος), also shady with sand and shingle, good for snorkelling. When we were there it was rather dirty but we gathered that it would be cleaned on that magic day, June 1. Round a bit further is **Christos** (Χρίστος) beach, near the church of the Transfiguration (Metamorphosis), pebbly, no shade, and further round still is **Helena** (Ελένα) beach of similar type. These last two you could find yourself sharing with some of the many goats on the island. Visiting these beaches constitutes a pleasant walk of about an hour each way.

To the north of the island the most popular beach is **Platys Yialos** (Πλατύς Γιαλός), about a hour's walk from Lipsi town. This is sandy with some shade from trees, and an excellent taverna, nominally open from June 1 but luckily it was open by mid May this year. Other beaches on this coast tend to get rubbish swept in from the sea, but the walks along it are good with spectacular views. To the east **Kamares** (Καμάρες) has shade, **Monodendri** (Μονοδέντρι) with its single tree, **Tourkomnima**, (Τουρκομνήμα) sand and shade, **Xirokambos** (Ξηρόκαμπος), **Hohlakoura** (Χοχλακούρα) no shade, except for one cave. In the south is **Katsadia** (Κατσαδία), about 35 minutes walk from the town and a popular beach, partly sand with shade, with a taverna in season. There is some accommodation here. We walked to most of these beaches, but swam only at Liendou as we like to travel light when we walk.

An excellent walk was along a donkey track across the island to the **Church of the Five Martyrs** above **Kimisi** (Κοίμηση) beach. Five monks were massacred by the Turks and their remains are in a casket in the church. The place is a haven of peace with a flower-filled garden, peacocks and tortoises. There are also memorials to local monks, priests, mayors and other worthies. It is possible to walk down from here to Kimissi beach down a very steep road or a slightly treacherous track. There are two chapels here, Upper and Lower Kimisi, which a hermit, Philippos, used to tend until 1999 when the new road disturbed his peace. He moved to the town and sadly died there in 2002.

Another church of note is the big town church of St John Theologos, financed partly by the Lipsians who emigrated to the USA. It contains the 'Black Virgin' icon, reputedly discovered in a tree indicated by a ray of light. The church was built on this spot. There is also the church of Panaghia tou Harou (Virgin of Death), near Hohlakoura. During the 1st World War lilies were placed on the icon of the Virgin holding Christ on the cross. The lilies died, but a year later new buds appeared, and supposedly do every year. A big festival is held on 22nd August when they process from the main church (where the icon is now kept) to its original home. The island is dotted with over 40 small churches, nearly all blue and white. From one viewpoint I counted 15.

Parts of the island are very fertile, with vines, olives, vegetables and some corn grown. The many goats produce a distinctive cheese, and surprisingly there are some cattle too. Honey is another local product from bees feasting on the abundant herbs and flowers. It is also good to see a number of horses and donkeys still used for transport.

Lipsi receives its usual quota of pick-up trucks arriving with various wares to sell: tablecloths, clothes, chairs, etc. There was one lorry filled with huge

earthenware pots (pithoi); in the centre was a space for the family to sit, and at the back strings of garlic and some potted plants. The trick, we heard, was not to buy until just before they were about to board the ferry again, when prices would be reduced.

There are several small islands around Lipsi, accessible on various trips. Recommended is the 'Five Island Trip' on Rena II, a beautiful caique. We first went to **Makronisi**, (Μακρονήσι) to the south, to swim off the boat. The intrepid can swim under an arch in the rock. Then up to the **Aspronissia** (Ασπρονήσια), pure white islands as the name suggests, where it is possible to swim to the shore, then to **Tiganakia** (Τηγανάκια) a group of tiny islands near **Arki** (Αρκοί) to the north, for a third swim. Next a coffee break at one of the 3 tavernas round a flower filled plateia on the harbourside of Arki. From there you proceed to another small island, **Marathi** (Μαράθι), for lunch in one of its three tavernas. On a second boat trip we spent longer at Marathi with time for lunch, a swim in the

Photo by David Leigh

beautiful sandy bay and exploration of the deserted village. (See next article for more about Arki and Marathi)

From Lipsi you can easily visit Leros to the south and Patmos to the north west, each boat trip taking just half an hour.

If you enjoy walking, swimming and the atmosphere of a truly traditional island, you would enjoy Lipsi. If you want sophistication and night clubs, don't go there.

How to get to Lipsi

By Air - Scheduled flights via Athens to nearby Samos or Kos, or charter flights direct to Samos or Kos then ferry.

By Ferry - Links with Agathonisi, Arki, Kalymnos, Kos, Leros, Patmos, Piraeus, Rhodes, Samos, Symi.

Package Tour Operators - Greek Sun, Hidden Greece, Island Wandering.

Tranquil Agathonisi, Arki & Marathi *by Peter Peacock*

Tranquil - serene, calm, undisturbed - that's **Agathonisi** (Αγαθονήσι), the most northerly of the Dodecanese, north east of Patmos and close to Turkey.

We left Gatwick on a charter flight direct to Samos arriving at 1 pm. A taxi took us to Pythagorio in plenty of time to catch the 2.30 pm ferry bound, eventually, for Kalymnos. Once on board I headed for the cafeteria and armed with a cheese pie and a can of Mythos sat on deck in the sunshine savouring them. The ferry crossing to Agathonisi took about an hour and on the way we spotted a pod of dolphins. What a way to start your holiday!

Formerly called Hyetousa, and in Medieval times Gaidaro, Agathonisi is a waterless lump of rock with about 110 inhabitants who make their living from farming, fishing, building and tourism within its 13 km². In 1821 Georgios Giameous from Patmos rented Agathonisi from the Turks and today's inhabitants are probably descended from Patmos and Fourni Greeks. It had electricity and telephone connections laid in 1984-5 when a new jetty was also built. Seven kilometres of concrete roads now connect most areas of the island and in 1992 a helipad was completed.

Our first visit to Agathonisi was in June 2000, when we were both employed by others and it used to take me at least three days of holiday to unwind and become more human, but within half a day here I was so relaxed I was almost horizontal. We were two of twelve land based tourists at the time and the only British. The only evidence of tourism then was a small wooden kiosk, a bit like a phone box, on the jetty which had a couple of postcards, plates and mugs, but was never open. It is still there now and is painted every year, but still never open when we are there in June. There is now, however, a post office/café bar on the jetty which, when open, sells T-shirts (only medium and small), post cards, pens, lighters, fridge magnets, etc. You can even send faxes from here.

Entering the Port of **Agios Georgios** (Αγ.Γεώργιος) is breathtaking and entertaining. The vibrant colours of flowers and plants enhance the view of village houses and tavernas laid out in a semi circle before you, just one row deep. The ferry does a three point

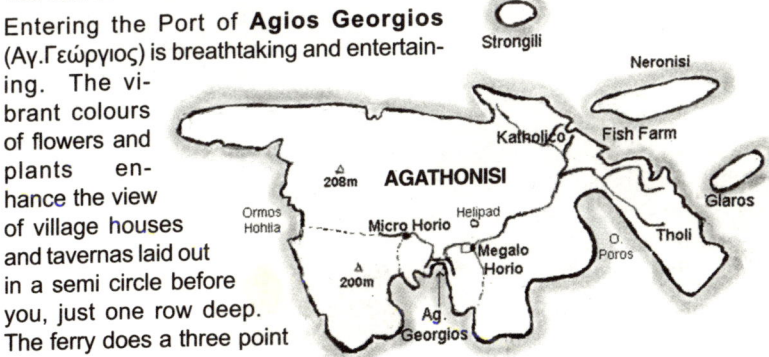

turn and backs onto the quay, anchors are dropped and the crew throw ropes ashore attached to what look like tennis balls, which are usually caught by a dog on the quayside. The boat is secured

before the usual frenetic activity of people, cars, trucks, parcels, machinery and animals getting on and off, lots of shouting and arm waving and then, suddenly, the ferry is gone. If you don't have accommodation prearranged, the boat is usually met by two ladies (Maria Kamitzi and Theologia Giameou) neither of whom speak much English, but enough to let their rooms. You'd put money on Maria coming away with a tourist or two!

Walking around the quayside to our room we were warmly greeted by the locals who remembered us from last year. Our accommodation this year was a room over Café Yetoza which has a magnificent balcony and excellent harbour and sea views.

There are just two other villages on the island, **Megalo Horio** and **Micro Horio**, but most visitors stay in the Ag. Georgios harbour area. The 'big' and 'little' Horios are accessible via concrete roads, up fairly steep hills. The only way to get around is on foot as there are no taxis or buses.

The harbour area has one mini-market and three family run tavernas, all offering good home cooked, mostly locally grown food, with goat being the speciality. You can still go into the kitchens and see what's cooking. George's Taverna, closest to the ferry terminal, has fantastic fish. His German wife, Sabina, cooks very good 'big beans' in tomato sauce and his sister also helps out. Limnaki and the mini-market are owned by Babis Kypraios who started by selling water melons and now has three businesses including another mini-market in Megalo Horio. Limnaki is frequented by many locals and the barbecued pork steaks and fish are wonderful. The Glaros (Sea gull) Taverna is owned and run by Yiannis and Voula Kopaniaris. Here Voula's mum normally cooks the dish of the day (I recommend her lemon chicken) and dad does the barbecue.

There are a couple of cafés - the more established Café Yetoza offers breakfast, lunchtime and evening snacks. Owner Vangelis is a fisherman in the winter but he often catches atherina (whitebait) in the summer and usually has an octopus in the fridge. The coastguards usually camp out here and are very interesting to talk to. The new café at a road junction appeals to the youngsters. It has an elevated wooden seating platform just across the road which looks a bit rickety with no guard rails (sorry, I'm a Safety Consultant!).

The shingle beach used by tourists and locals, has a pleasant family feel, or you can head out of the village, past the swings and take the left hand track to Spilia Beach, a pebble beach with a cave and crystal clear water. We nicknamed this Duck Bay because it is where three ducks live, when they are not visiting the harbour area. They're a minor tourist attraction.

There are pleasant walks with spectacular views around the island - left or right from the harbour it's just 15-20 minutes to Micro or Megalo Horio respectively. After Micro Horio you can continue through farmland to **Hohlia Bay** (Ο. Χοχλιά) and eventually the small stony cove of **Giadouravlakos** beach. To the southwest is an area called **Tholi** (Θόλοι) which has a fish farm, a small sandy tamarisk lined cove called **Poros** (Πόρος), Byzantine ruins and the pretty little fishing harbour of **Katholico** (Καθολικό) where fishermen mend their nets and shelter from the winds.

Ruins at Tholi

When you don't want to walk, there are always people or boats to entertain you. It can be amusing watching as yachts anchor up and the tourist 'sailors' come ashore. It is even more fun to watch them go back after a meal and a few bottles of retsina or ouzo. You may get the odd 'big ship' moor up - a Greek Naval Ship, the coastguard or the 'Fruit and Vog' boat (a converted fishing boat bringing supplies) or the night time Water Boat. One time the ferry trapped its

anchor on the rocks and it took over an hour to free it. There is always something to observe and chuckle at.

Agathonisi is a wonderful little island where the local people are very helpful and friendly. When it comes to tourism they are not really commercially minded. I was in two minds whether to write about the island as it doesn't deserve to be spoilt by hordes of tourists, but some locals I consulted felt it may help to have a few more tourists (and Greek-o-File readers are the more appreciative kind - Ed). Day tourist boats occasionally pitch up from Samos and at weekends private boats arrive too. Many locals don't speak English so it can be fun communicating and trying out your Greek.

We enjoyed a week on Agathonisi before catching the ferry heading west to Arki, just a few kilometres north of Lipsi.

Arriving at the island of **Arki** (Αρκοί) on the Nissos Kalymnos ferry used to be a nightmare. You'd have to tell the captain you wanted to land there and a caique would be sent out to meet you. Transferring from the ferry to the caique could be dodgy. Now, however, they have a ferry terminal with shade (one umbrella!) and a mostly concreted road leading to the village (about 400 metres, a 10 minutes walk). The whole island is only 7 km².

Three times a week a small boat (The Lambi) arrives from Patmos, bringing supplies and people, and also visiting Marathi and Lipsi. The village is centred around the little harbour overlooked by three tavernas - Manolis (very Greek), O Trypas and Nikolas (family run) and all have rooms too. Manolis sometimes meets the boat, Nikolas has stunning views over the harbour and Trypas just up the hill is very arty.

The kiosk on the harbour front sells cigarettes, ice cream, drinks and tourist stuff. If you can't get a room, ask here and they'll help you. The mini market is about 200 metres up the hill and to the left, but the tavernas will sell you

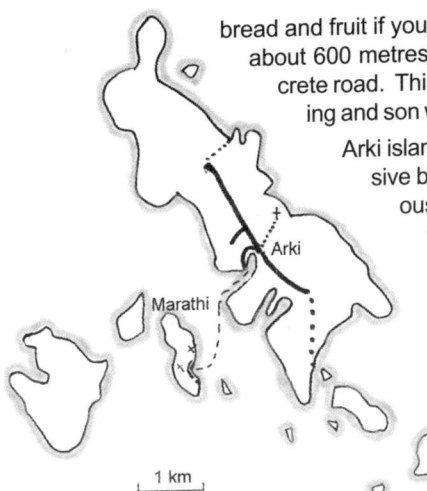

bread and fruit if you wish. A fourth taverna, Abelaki, is about 600 metres after Nikolas Taverna on the concrete road. This family run outfit with mother cooking and son waiting is well worth the gentle walk.

Arki island has its own generator and a massive bank of solar panels. There are various walks to small beaches, but the footpaths are not well signed so it can be a bit of a cross country ramble. Arki is a very friendly, quiet and laid back island now, but I heard there are plans afoot to 'develop' this small island, so get there soon before the high rises appear.

Disembarking at one of the two small jetties either end of the 350 metre sandy bay of the tiny island of **Marathi** (Μαράθι), just a short hop away, is a bit like landing on a tropical island. The Lambi, coming from Patmos via Arki, etc drops you off at around 11.30 am, returns about 1 pm and leaves at 2 pm, giving you time for lunch on a day trip, or to find accommodation if you fancy staying. One little quirk about the island is the electricity generator which is switched off at 11 pm and not turned on again until 9 am. It can be quite romantic!

Marathi's three tavernas, at the only settlement which is beside the beach, also have accommodation available. Pandelis is very up-market and commercially minded (€45+ per room per night in June 2006, compared with

€25-30 for the others). Stavrangos in the middle is run by the new boy, Stavros Kavouras, aged 64. His cousin, Mikaelis Kavouras, dresses and looks like a pirate and operates the Marathi Taverna at the other end of the beach. Along with his brother and sister they are the only inhabitants who live there all year round. The island food is excellent with lots of local chicken and goat on the menu.

The ruins of the old village and the local church lie behind the Marathi Taverna, up a winding footpath. On the way up you pass a tree with metal hooks hanging from it - this is the slaughter 'house'! The ruins of 8 dwellings can still be seen along with a circle of stones used for threshing corn. The only transport on the island is the dumper truck which drives along the narrow jetty to off-load supplies from the boat and then reverses all the way back with its load. They say nothing has fallen off yet.

Apart from the usual people watching, we were often entertained by Sambica, an island dog who likes to catch fish in the sea. He stands perfectly still in the shallow water until the fish swim around him, then plunges his head in, invariably coming up with a fish.

Sambica fishing by small jetty

A small arts and crafts shop is run by a Dutch guy who comes to stay every summer and around the headland a research station is used by visiting marine biologists and environmentalists who also have a base on Arki.

Marathi is a beautiful and magical place to visit and well worth stopping for at least a couple of days if you appreciate tranquillity.

How to get to Agathonisi, Arki & Marathi

By Air - Scheduled or charter to Athens, Samos or Kos - then ferry

By Ferry - to/from Kalymnos, Leros, Lipsi, Patmos, Samos - and each other

Package Tour Operators - these islands are really only for independent tourists, but possibly available on request with a holiday to nearby islands.

Mediterranean Cruise Eclipsed *by Tony Davis*

The highlight of 2006 was, for us, a holiday to eclipse all others!

We flew to Iraklion, Crete, a few days before the big event in March, had a look round Knossos (which had changed only a little since our previous visit many moons previously) then boarded our cruise ship, which chugged off at about midnight.

It was no floating mega-glitz-palace affair, but held about 700 passengers and was Greek-run. The food was excellent, service also, cabin tiny, sunbathing great (though often chilly) and the lectures mostly pretty good - covering histories of the places we visited as well as the astronomy of eclipses.

We docked at Benghazi, Libya on our second night and the following morning visited Greek and Roman ruins at Cyrene. Morning - did I say? Well, by the time our 18 coaches managed to get to the destination - what with refuelling, loo stops and negotiating narrow hilly winding roads (in beautiful rolling green country), with police escort and ambulances - it was after noon when we arrived.

The site was fascinating and very picturesque. We were left to wander about on our own with no clear idea about when to return to the coaches. The loo was revolting, but I managed to splash out al fresco in a semi-secluded corner of some architectural ruin! (This was a venture to be repeated on subsequent trips - in fact there was no seclusion at all at our wide-open eclipse site the next day, 500 km south in the Libyan desert.)

Collecting us all for the return to the ship was shambolic, with no guaranteed method of ensuring no-one was left stranded. (Refuelling was even worse on the return trip - only one pump was available for the 18 coaches.) A repeat performance on the eclipse trip the next morning would mean we would not get a proper view of the great event. Mega management panic! The solution was to allow an extra 2 hours for the journey - *ie* set off at 3 am !! Come March 26, this we did, but still could not arrive soon enough for some of the astro gizmos to be set up, which was seriously bad news for some of the party.

However, the big event itself went off exactly to plan. The Moon arrived exactly on cue, did its stuff and slid off without a hitch, with no interference from clouds (of which there was not the merest puff to be seen). It was a truly wonderful eclipse - 4 minutes and 11 seconds of totality - and I managed to get some OK photographs.

A leisurely 2-day cruise then took us to Leptis Magna, near Tripoli - a magnificent vast Roman site with sea views thrown in for extra interest. Then more *very* leisurely cruising, sunbathing, scoffing, boozing and making new acquaintances - until three mornings later there were gasps of amazement at the stunning sight of the west coast of ... Thira !

People who had never seen it before were totally gobsmacked - and even those of us who had (as Lorraine and I had) were held in awe at that great 900 feet of almost sheer cliff, dark brown with a wide streak of white ash and with white buildings atop. It looked like a huge chocolate cake with brilliant white icing. I've always thought the ancient name, Thira, more appropriate to this view than the more benign, Italianate Santorini.

Our coaches zig-zagged up the hairpin bends and squeezed along the narrow roads, taking us on a guided tour of the island, with some very acceptable wine tasting thrown in. On being left then to our own devices, we wandered at leisure, dawdled over lunch, took the cable car down to the minuscule port, dawdled yet more over ouzo, wine, coffee, salad, raki, this and that, before being conveyed back to the ship.

As on previous nights, the ship's forward deck lights were doused to reveal a brilliant display of stars, dominated by an impressive Jupiter.

Next morning Piraeus, a quick dash to the Parthenon, flashes of lightning only a short distance to the north, big claps of thunder, lots of people, school parties, etc, etc, then the airport, Heathrow and home.

Great trip! When's the next one?

Profile of Kythnos *by Sylvia Cook*

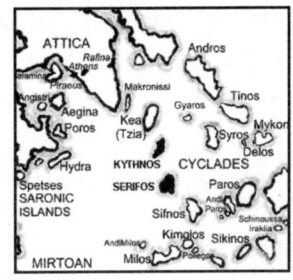

North of Serifos and south of Kea, the island of **Kythnos** (Κύθνος) is the first Cycladic island from Piraeus on several ferry routes. Just 99km² of mostly barren limestone rock, the main port of **Merihas** (Μέριχας) is well connected by bus to both the inland traditional towns - **Kythnos Town** and **Dryopida** (Δρυοπίδα), the hot mineral springs at **Loutra** (Λουτρά) on the north east coast and the quiet beach and monastery at **Panaghia Kanala** (Παναγία Κανάλα) in the south east. Small beaches and hidden coves are dotted around the coastline and animals graze on the slopes above.

Kythnos Background

☐ *Evidence of habitation between 7500 - 6600BC near Loutra is the oldest in this part of the Aegean. In ancient times it was known as Dryopis after the Dryopes settlers from Evvia. Also known as Thermia since 1143 and to many Greeks today, due to its therapeutic thermal springs.*

☐ *Generally following the fortunes of nearby islands, the Italian Gozodini family were given Kythnos in 1337 remaining until 1579, when the Turks took power.*

☐ *In the 19th c. the island economy was boosted by patients flocking to the hot springs at Loutra - said to be beneficial for those with arthritis and bone disorders. The Loutra bath house is still popular today.*

Adapted from Road
Editions Road Atlas,
Island map also avail.

☐ *One of the first modern Greek wind farms was built east of Kythnos Town in 1982, to take advantage of incessant strong winds.*

A Close Hop from Athens by Sylvia Cook

As they are adjoining Cycladic islands close to the mainland, we planned an island hop around Kea, Kythnos and possibly Serifos - although no ferries nor island rooms were booked in spite of trying. The only prices we could find for accommodation on Kea or Kythnos on the internet were high. Surely things could not have changed *that* much since our last Cycladic holiday in 1999! We made a note of some listings with no email details and hoped they or others would be cheaper on arrival early in September 2006.

Anticipating costs is a worry when travelling independently, so I make no apology for mentioning prices frequently for this trip. Low season holidays can work out cheaper prearranged with tour operators, but destinations are limited. However you don't always get what you pay for with individual internet suppliers and 'a bird in the hand' at the port can drive a harder bargain.

Surprisingly, the port of Lavrion has not yet extended its services greatly, although it is closer to the Cyclades than Piraeus. Perhaps it is unable to take the large ferries that dock at Piraeus. It was easy to get to on an early bus from the airport after our overnight flight from Heathrow. We shared the bus with just one other passenger, who clearly knew the bus driver. We seemed to make a slight detour, to drop him off, before going on to Lavrion.

I'd forgotten about the strong winds in these parts. It was very blustery and a little cold as we waited outside the small port café kiosk until it opened at 7.30am, then drank our metrio coffees to warm and wake up. The crossing from here was just an hour to **Kea** (Κέα) also known as **Tzia** (Τζιά) and as we arrived at **Korissia** (Κορησία) harbour it appeared to have all that we wanted from a Greek island - a small resort area with a few cafe bars and tavernas, a long sandy beach - so you might be wondering why there is no Profile of Kea here! Well, we didn't really see much of it.

There were no welcoming 'rooms' people and no interest shown in our arrival at the cafés along the front as we towed our small cases, obviously looking for somewhere to stay. On asking we were directed to the end of the village and inland along a dry river road, where a number of establishments were either fully let or expensive, eventually finding an available room at 'United Europe'. Asking for a cheap room, the proprietor enquired what we wanted to pay, so we said about €20 (as a bargaining figure). He laughed and said €40 was the best he would do. We took it for one night initially, saying we'd let him know if we would stay longer. It was an OK room, with a fridge and 2 hotplates, but no plug in the washbasin and only a tiny shower, albeit with a curtain, but nothing special and a fair walk from the beach. The door rate was €65. We'd prebooked a central Athens double room including breakfast at €39 for the end of our stay, so it really was overpriced.

Rechecking ferry times to Kythnos, it seemed that we would have to stay either 1 or 4 nights before we could move on. The tour offices could not help with rooms. We telephoned one place in **Ioulis** (Ιουλίς), the inland Hora, but they still wanted €35 for a room with no fridge. We would probably want to be at the coast some of the time, buses were now geared to school times not the 'high season' timetable, and a single night's stay was finally decided when we ordered a light lunch of a horiatiki to share (tiny portion) and two beers for €16 at the cheapest establishment we could find. This place obviously didn't want visitors. We rang ahead to a contact number on Kythnos and easily booked a double room with fridge, etc for €25 per night, so bought tickets for the morning ferry to leave this unfriendly isle.

When we later told our landlord that we were leaving early in the morning for a €25 per night room on Kythnos, he said they were more hungry on Kythnos - but perhaps they are just more greedy in Korissia.

However, I had wanted to see the ancient lion and Ioulis so in the early evening we found a taxi driver (who turned out to be George, recommended on Matt Barrett's website). The walk through the village and out the other side on a cobbled path was rewarded with views across to the recumbent, smiling **Lion of Kea**, hewn from the rocks circa 600BC. There were no other visitors so we could get really close to contemplate the amiable feline.

Our evening in the traditional Hora, Ioulis, was more our style too, wandering through the narrow streets (see front cover), having an early evening ouzo, gavros fish, *patatas* and *salata* at Rolando's (for only €2 more than our light lunch in Korissia), before returning by taxi for an expensive ouzo nightcap.

Early next morning we set off for **Kythnos**, viewing the Kea coast from aboard as we breakfasted on rolls and cheese from the Kea bakery. The sun was warm, but as we passed the end of the island strong winds cut across the gap between the islands. We approached **Merihas** slowly as the harbour was busy and had time to look around the sandy beach of **Kolonna** along the spit connecting the islet of **Ag. Loukas**. Although there is an old 'eyesore' derelict concrete hotel at the opposite end from the harbour, generally it came across as a laid back and unpretentious resort village.

We soon found our landlady, Panayiota, via her nephew's travel office near the harbour and she trundled up on her little quad bike, took our luggage

and led us at a walking pace to her rooms, just back from the bridge over the 'river' road. The room was clean, small and had everything we needed at a good price. We quickly unpacked and set off to explore.

There was a butcher, a baker, 4 small supermarkets, and a good few small tavernas and bars to choose from (but no obvious locals' kafeneion), a harbour and fishing boats, but no beach. We found beer, bread and salad for a balcony lunch and in the afternoon set off to walk to nearby **Martinakia** beach. It was a sandy, tamarisk backed beach sloping gently out to sea, small but not crowded on 8th September, although surprisingly the 2 tavernas had already closed down - a situation we found in many places where most business is from Greek tourists in the short school holiday season.

In the evening the stroll from the harbour to the opposite end of the bay, past the ugly hotel, found us the best price for a preprandial beer (€2, other tavernas €2.5 minimum, bars more) but local wine was generally a good buy at €3 for a *miso kilo* in many places and

food prices fairly average.

Miles Lambert Gócs commented on the symmetry of Kythnos' bus routes in his gastronomic tour of Greece in 'Greek Salad' and he was right. We were there on the cusp of timetable changes, but in spite of some variations to the times posted, it was still easy to take in all we hoped to see. The next morning we headed south - just 15 minutes later stopping in the picturesque old village of **Dryopida**, continuing through fairly barren hillsides dotted with small churches, derelict and converted old windmills. I felt this evidence of the harnessing of wind power in previous centuries sat comfortably with a row of modern wind turbines on a ridge in the distance behind us.

Arriving at **Panagia Kanala** in the south east, we alighted outside the monastery and walked down though a pine clad slope to test the beach - peaceful, mostly sandy, with a few 'rooms for rent' and two closed tavernas. Returning to the top there were more signs of life, including an open cafe/souvlaki bar where we relaxed over a Greek coffee and chatted with the owner before returning to the monastery to await our bus back to **Dryopida**.

Once there we wandered around stone-paved narrow streets between white-washed houses, unusually with red tiled roofs in this part of the island. We came across the open door of a small folk museum. Entry was free and no one was inside this traditional village house with just 3 small rooms displaying old kitchen tools, agricultural implements, a spinning wheel, weaving loom (see front cover) and old costumes. I'm not sure if we found the cave with underground lake, but we did venture down some steps to a dark tunnel, signposted as caves near the new tiny open air theatre, deciding against further exploration in the dark.

A friendly greeting from a lady cleaning tables at a cafe set behind the main taverna area encouraged us to go back to 'Το Σοκακι' (meaning backstreet) for a lunchtime beer and €5 pikilia, after we'd explored a local minimarket and bought loose olives. It was a long wait for food as 'mum' went to get her 'daughter' who had to visit the shop before cooking our plate of tasty titbits. We did get chatting to Viktor who appeared from the rooms above and introduced himself as the husband of the lady who had first greeted us. Other relationships are just guessed - but we like to while away time speculating. Although a leisurely lunch, we were still in time for our bus back to Merihas before the afternoon siesta.

Next day was lazy, spent at Merihas, with a walk to Martinakia beach again. By the following day we were ready for the other bus expedition, north to **Loutra**. As with similar health-giving spas in Greece, doctors will give patients a prescription to use the waters. We went straight to the utilitarian low block building to investigate the baths and queued with the mostly elderly people for our tickets. No English was spoken, but the lady who showed us to our separate bath cubicles explained with hand signs that she would knock on our door when our 20 minutes was nearing completion and we must pull out the plug to empty the bath before drying and getting dressed.

It was a strange, somewhat surreal experience relaxing up to my neck in buoyant warm water in the deep marble, stained bath with only dripping water and silence for company, sun filtering through the tiny windows high above, but I did feel invigorated later.

Loutra seemed to exist only for visitors to its thermal springs. The hotels inevitably appeared to cater for elderly clientele, or well heeled ones. The Yacht Club price list showed €5 for a beer. We rehydrated with soft drinks from a minimarket and sat on a wall overlooking the marina. Wandering around the bay to investigate a modern turreted building, we came across a Greek lady in swimsuit sat astride a warm stream with her back to the flowing water, presumably to ease some problem. We traced the stream back to where it emerged from a rock near the bathhouse - was it a separate natural spring, or was our water getting a second use!

Back to Hora on the 1.30pm bus, it didn't seem particularly attractive from the road. However, away from the bus stop a myriad of narrow streets, painted with white lines and flowers, led off through whitewashed, blue-shuttered houses with bougainvillea in abundance, potted flowers, pavement cafes and all that you would expect from a Cycladic Hora.

Sat outside a kafeneion in a narrow street, we felt refreshed and ready for our return to Merihas - on foot. We could have taken a bus but it was time to get some exercise and maybe visit a beach on the way back. The road wound down the hill slopes and there were no obvious footpaths cutting across so we stayed on the quiet road most of the way down to **Episkopi** (Επισκοπή). Along the way we saw ladies collecting large bunches of ripe grapes from unkempt, seemingly wild vines beside the road. *"Orea stafilia!"* commented Terry. The ladies smiled and insisted we took a bunch to enjoy on our way.

For the energetic, a walk to **Apokrisi** beach possibly continuing to the sandy **Kolonna** beach, returning via Episkopi would be feasible, but perhaps not for us. The morning bus had passed near the southern end of Episkopi beach and I'd seen a taverna there, so this was our planned stopping place. A track down the side of a valley towards some holiday homes cut off the last hairpin bend, but ended with a scramble down to the beach where roadworks were incomplete. We eagerly trekked the length of the sandy beach to find yet another closed taverna! It was a little gusty to enjoy the fine sandy beach, but we rested there a while, enjoying some of the sweet grapes, before continuing our trek back to Merihas via our now regular beach, Martinakia.

Our remaining food supplies provided a small meze on our balcony before a *volta* to the souvlaki bar at the far end for just a light meal - but it had closed for the season. We went again to Byzantio which had been our favourite eating place and I ordered 'carbonara' but ate very little. It was delicious, but I was not really hungry and Terry had more than enough for himself. The waiter insisted on piling it into a foil container to takeaway, although I explained we were leaving next day. I didn't like to 'bin' it, but a friendly dog at the harbour saved the day and wolfed it down straight from its foil dish. I think he enjoyed his 'doggy' bag.

After Kea, Kythnos had been a breath of fresh air. There was a friendly welcome and plenty for us to enjoy, with enough places to go to for those who like nothing better than doing nothing and exploring the nowheres of off-the-beaten-track rural Greece. September travellers should be prepared for many out of town places being closed though.

Panayiota said why not stay longer as we thanked her and left after our 4 nights. We thought we might return if we didn't like to Serifos.

Profile of Serifos *by Sylvia Cook*

Adapted from Road Editions Road Atlas, Island map also avail.

South of Kythnos and northwest of Sifnos, **Serifos** (Σέριφος) is a little smaller at 73 km² and also fairly barren, although there is some agriculture. The traditional white sugarcube houses of **Serifos Hora** sit impressively on a steep sided hill, topped with a Venetian kastro,

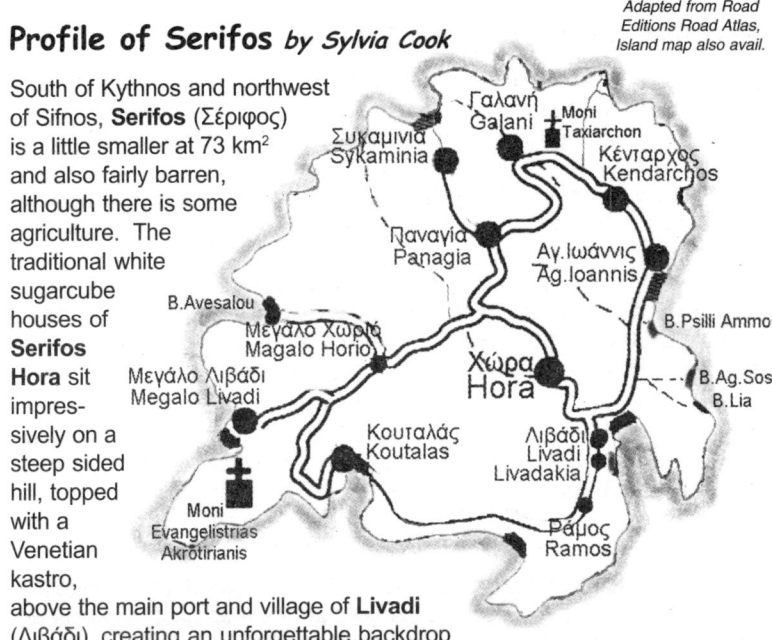

above the main port and village of **Livadi** (Λιβάδι), creating an unforgettable backdrop from most points of the wide U-shaped bay. Serifos boasts a number of sandy beaches, mostly accessible from dirt roads, or by boat. The oldest island church, built 950AD is at the village of **Panaghia** (Παναγία).

Serifos Background

❐ *In mythology the young Perseus was washed ashore on Serifos in a chest with his mother Danäe (despatched by her father after an oracle said he would be killed by her son). The king Polydectes desired and pursued the beautiful Danäe, but she was not interested. When Perseus grew up the king sent him off on impossible missions to improve his wooing chances. Perseus returned with the severed head of Medusa which he showed to the king and his court - who were all turned to stone, as was the island.*

❐ *Ancient Serifos was a relatively rich island, presumably partly due to the opencast iron mines worked first by Ionian settlers. It fell out of favour with Rome and became a place for exiles, causing its decline.*

❐ *Intensive mining since 1867 brought prosperity again, but in 1916 local labourers revolted in **Megalo Livadi** (Μεγάλο Λιβάδι) demanding an 8-hour working day. Four lives were lost when the protest was violently overthrown. The mines became non-profitable and closed in 1964.*

Next Stop, Serifos *by Sylvia Cook*

Setting off on another windy ferry journey, particularly gusty between the islands, we telephoned ahead for rooms before arriving at **Serifos'** **Livadi** harbour. One said €40 per night, another €30, but Margarita's said €25, although we did not make the booking. The port looked wonderful on our arrival midday. Some minibuses meeting the ferry were asking €30, but that was for studios at nearby Livadakia. As we walked along the front heading for the far end to find Margarita's, we were propositioned several times, mostly offering higher priced accommodation. Then again by a pretty young lady with good English, so I replied *"only if you have a cheap room"* - sometimes it's best not to try Greek. She said €20, so we went to look, up a narrow side street at 'Anastasia - rooms and studios'.

The room was small but fine, included a fridge, basic facilities and a tiny lookout-balcony above the narrow street. There were studios available for €10 more. We only prepare the odd salad, sandwich or meze with drinks, so took the small room for the first night before committing to longer as we were concerned about possible late night noise from two music bars at the top end of the street (but they were not especially loud, early or late).

It was certainly ideally placed for access to all parts of Livadi, which stretched around a large deep bay from the harbour at one end, past moorings for yachts and fishing boats, waterside tavernas and bars, a few shops, gradually thinning out with hotels and a firm sandy beach disappearing into the distance. As you walk along the front, you see Serifos Hora from most places, topped with a kastro and with whitewashed houses tumbling down the slopes of the hill behind - possibly the most picturesque harbour and

Livadi & Hora, Serifos (in colour on front cover)

hora setting I've seen in Greece. We loved Livadi and stayed there our maximum 5 days before we had to leave for Athens.

A couple of our subscribers had mentioned that they would be on Serifos in September, so we'd noted their hotel 'just in case'. We found it on our first exploration walkabout and left a card with message, returning in the evening. Derek and Liz were there at the suggested time so we joined them for an evening drink followed by a meal. They had a hire car and kindly offered to take us on an island tour the next day.

Setting off to the east, we looked down on beaches from the road high above **Lia** (Λιά), **Sosti** (Σώστη) and **Psili Ammos** (Ψιλή Άμμος), all picturesque with little habitation around. Derek said the sand was fine and soft, but the taverna at the latter had closed. The recently surfaced road (not on our maps) must have been above the village of **Kendarchos** (Κένδαρχος) which we did not find, although we did pass its white Taxiarchos monastery. Having tried a few on previous excursions, Derek felt that some of the tracks off this road were not good for small hire cars, so we continued on the main road bypassing **Galani** (Γαλανή) too without seeing it until we looked back. When we stopped to look down the road to **Sykaminia** (Συκαμινιά), which looked good for a walk, the little road down to **Panaghia** was also visible, so we turned off the main road and parked at the top of this little inland village to explore the narrow streets.

Many of the small houses were derelict, but there were also renovated houses. We moved aside to let a mule train of two pass by, with sand and cement in panniers, on its way to a rebuild project at the end. As we watched them unload, Terry remarked to the lady overseeing the workers that building must be difficult here. She agreed and said everything must be carried by mule. As we sipped our coffees in the little village kafeneion later and nibbled on the hard dry cheese and bread which came with our coffee order, we watched them pass a few more times and reflected on the acceptance of this slow, simple life without modern technology and gadgets.

Megalo Livadi was our next stop. It has a very pretty bay with waves lapping the narrow sandy beach, two tavernas, two rows of trees and behind was a crumbling disused mansion house and a sprinkling of habitation. The two tavernas looked similar, so we checked out the more empty one (very reasonable) and enjoyed a meze of '*orektika*', intending to have a light lunch but leaving to explore replete and refreshed by the calmness of this seaside village.

It is a fascinating coastal village with an interesting recent history evident all around us. A memorial to those who lost their lives in the 1916 strike added a poignancy to the signs of the now defunct mining industry - the once smart mansion house evoked pictures of the gentry profiteering from downtrod-

den workers; the rusting gantry further round the coast, where the raw material of their labours was loaded on ships from the now corroded railway trucks still sitting on the old rails. There was no explanation on the site - but somehow this added to the experience. You had to stop and take in what you could see and feel to imagine what had been.

Further round the coast, the bay of **Koutalas** (Κουταλάς) looked inviting as we approached, but up close was hard packed sand. **Ganema** (Γάνεμα) beach nearby looked softer, although being a windy day we decided against testing the water and beach. The tarmac road ended at this point, so we retraced our tracks to before Panaghia and turned right to drive past the Hora (stopping of course for photographs) on our return to Livadi. First our guide for the day took us to inspect **Livadakia** which had a better beach than Livadi, but was surrounded by more modern and touristy accommodation and lacked the village feel and atmosphere of Livadi.

Derek and Liz dropped us back at the harbour at 4.30pm, just 6 hours after we had started our island tour - and we had stopped many times. After this island introduction we didn't feel the need to revisit anywhere other than the **Hora**. The prevailing wind was from the east, so although we had considered walking to nearby **Lia** beach, it seemed pointless as our long but narrow sandy beach was sheltered at the far end, had plenty of space to spread away from others, with easy access to tavernas, supermarkets and our room. We ventured to Livadakia beach one day just for interest, but there were more people there so any advantages, such as softer sand, were outweighed.

In need of relaxation for our last few days we soon settled in 'our' places - Almeriki, an ouzerie, was small, friendly, had good meze food and the cheapest booze (€1.5 ouzo, €2 big beer, €4 wine per litre, good coffee too) and Stamatos, a taverna between the beach and harbour so on the *volta* route any time of day, good traditional Greek fare and good prices. There may well have been other places we would have enjoyed, but there are advantages to doing a quick menu survey (preferably when 'greeters' aren't around), deciding where to try out, then settling on a couple of regular spots - not least because you get to know the staff and fellow clientele.

The trip up to Hora on the bus and walking back down was the easiest option and we enjoyed exploring the narrow streets between mostly reno-vated bijou houses of the upper village, the lower part seeming to have more local tenants. The views were spectacular from the top by the kastro, looking down over the massive bay where a small cruise ship had made an alternative stop (instead of Mykonos) to anchor in this sheltered harbour. Again many tavernas and coffee bars had closed for the season, the re-maining one in the plateia was crowded with cruise passengers at lunch-time *and* expensive, so we rested in a quiet spot with gorgeous views to enjoy refreshments from the minimarket, before taking the well signed foot-path downhill, cutting all the hairpin bends off the road route.

Soon after arrival we had tried to book our return to Piraeus on a fast boat to arrive in plenty of time to get to our Athens hotel, but all seats were taken and we were lucky to get booked on the slow big ferry due back at Piraeus quite late. It is worth noting, if possible do not plan to return to Piraeus on a Sunday as ferries are prebooked well in advance by Athenians who enjoy late summer weekends away from the city.

We met up with and enjoyed the company of Derek and Liz several times whilst on Serifos. They joined us for a last drink after we'd had an early evening plate of the plentiful atherinas at Almeriki, before going for our ferry. It was good to be 'seen off' waiting for our slightly delayed ferry, then waving from the deck when we spotted their faces amongst the masses below.

Livadi caters for all types, with enough space for different kinds of tourists to coexist and enjoy what they each want from their holidays - quiet bars or modern Greek music (not too loud), smarter restaurants or family tavernas, people-watching or soaking up sunrays. The island has old villages to ex-plore, ancient and modern history, plenty of churches, long hillside walks and deserted beaches. We also noticed that drivers here seemed more patient and less aggressive than we have seen in other parts of Greece. I definitely recommend Serifos for any lover of Greece.

How to get to Kythnos & Serifos

By Air - Scheduled or charter to Athens, then ferry

By Ferry - mainland Pireaus for both, Lavrio for Kythnos, connections with most Cycladic islands

Package Tour Operators -

Kythnos - Explore Worldwide, Hidden Greece, Island Wandering, Sunisle
Serifos - Elysian, Greek Sun, Hidden Greece, Island Wandering

The Morning Ferry *by Josie Jeffrey*

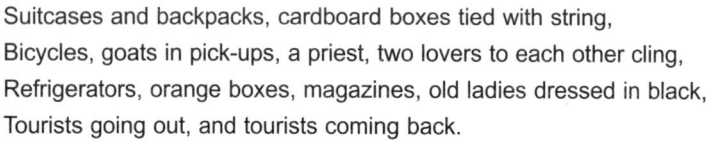

Early morning, fresh and new, save for the dark
    plume rising straight to windless sky,
The burning of the 'papers', day's first reminder
    that many others have passed by,
A dark exclamation mark hovers over this
    ancient rock,
As the ferry judders nearer, aiming slowly for the dock.

Suitcases and backpacks, cardboard boxes tied with string,
Bicycles, goats in pick-ups, a priest, two lovers to each other cling,
Refrigerators, orange boxes, magazines, old ladies dressed in black,
Tourists going out, and tourists coming back.

Lorries and mopeds, hire cars and wheelbarrows wait,
To collect precious cargo, newspapers, lipsticks, a TV in a crate,
The old trollop dancing, bumps and grinds her way to shore,
Discharges housewives laden from some far off department store.

Goodbyes and promises, helloes, hail friend well met,
And as the daily exchange takes place, you can surely bet,
When the old girl's hooter tells us that she's on her way,
Two ticket waving joggers will arrive, too late to leave today.

The island floats away from view, another's coming by,
And life ashore moves nearer, so I gather bags and sigh,
For the journey's nearly over that began in Athens' sultry dark,
As another timeless traveller, it's my turn to disembark.

Exploring Inland *by Graeme Dakin*

My early visits to Greece were limited to beach holidays and organised trips. As time moved on I was intrigued to know what lay beyond the coastal resorts and took to walking several miles inland to explore the countryside. This tended to be on roads which, in the hillier areas, involved walking lengthy distances along a series of hairpin bends to get to my destinations. Even so, it opened up a whole new world of wonderful landscapes, scenic vil-

lages, traditional kafeneions, colourful characters and exposure to a wide range of plants, animals and insects - such as this 'Kalymnian Blue' butterfly.

The Greek people seemed to appreciate my willingness to come away from the tourist areas and would often ask where I was heading, offering gifts of fruit to fuel my journey. A local in rural northwest Corfu showed a nice sense of humour when a fellow walker inadvertently greeted him with *"Kalamari"* rather than *"Kalimera"* by doing a highly comical impersonation of a squid! When visiting rural tavernas or kafeneions, I was pleasantly surprised at the 'village not tourist prices' charged. In one Crete taverna, after confirming that I was English, an elderly local insisted on paying for my meze and beer as a thank you for our support during the Second World War.

I thought it would be more enjoyable to walk on paths and tracks away from the roads to get even closer to nature. I became aware of the **Sunflower** series of 'Landscapes' books (www.sunflowerbooks.co.uk). These are an excellent source of information and aim *"to lure visitors away from the tourist centres and into the countryside"*. Each book in the series also includes car tours and picnic spot suggestions, but walks - from short strolls to long hikes - are the key feature. These cover many holiday areas and currently feature the following Greek destinations:

Corfu, Crete (Eastern) Crete (Western), Cyprus (Southern), Kefalonia, Lesvos, Paxos, Peloponnese (South), Rhodes & Samos.

As well as the walks (many of which can be reached using local buses) and detailed maps, the books include recommendations regarding what to take,

where to stay, best time of year for walking, weather, *"things that bite or sting"* and some useful Greek language for walkers. They also offer an on-line update service so that you can check if anything has happened to alter the viability of the walks and gather alternative directions supplied by other walkers. I found these guides really useful and own several of them. Because the walks themselves can be scattered over quite large geographical areas, you might need to hire a car to do several within one holiday.

I then became aware of a series of walking booklets produced by Lance Chilton of **Marengo Publications** (www.marengowalks.com). These focus on the immediate surrounding area of popular holiday resorts and so several walks can be done from your holiday base without worrying about transport. The booklets provide an overview of the local area and its facilities and history, before launching into the walks. Another positive feature is the impressive large scale folding maps that accompany most of these guides showing the walks themselves and many other useful geographical features. Currently the Greek destinations covered are:

Corfu Northwest (Arillas, Agios Georgios and Agios Stefanos); Crete East (Elounda), Crete North (Geogioupolis & Rethymnon), Crete South (Plakias); Mainland Parga, Pilion, Stoupa & Kardamyli; Kalymnos, Kos (Kamari & Kefalos), Lefkas & Meganisi (Nidri), Lesvos (Petra & Anaxos), Samos (Kokkari), Symi, Thassos (Skala Potamias and Golden Beach).

Lance is also an expert botanist and publishes 'Plant Checklists' for many of these destinations as well as offering a series of guided walks to a number of these resorts each year.

Other walking publications concentrating on a single area that I have found very useful are:

Lesvos - 'On Foot in North Lesvos' by Mike Maunder which details 26 walks in the Molyvos and Petra areas (available from several shops in these resorts).

Peloponnese (Mani) - 'Walking in Mani' by Mat Dean covering 10 walks close to the resorts of

A local cat patiently awaits the opening of a typical Lesvian village kafeneion.

Stoupa, Kardamyli and Agios Nikolaos (available from Bob Barrow's travel agency in Stoupa).

Crete (Apokoronas) - 'There and Back with Anna & Bob' outlining 5 walks in the Plaka/Almirida area. This booklet is available from the Papyrus bookshop in Kalives (a similar booklet is also available for walks in the Kalives area) and all proceeds go to the Royal National Institute for the Blind.

If you haven't ventured out into the Greek countryside, I encourage you to do so. If you are constructing your own walks, be aware of the extra demands that the higher temperatures will make and take plenty of water, apply lots of sunscreen and wear a hat. If following one of the documented walks, be realistic about your fitness level when considering the grade of the walk and follow the recommendations made regarding footwear, clothing, equipment etc. You will meet local characters who will brighten your day in some way and you will be richer for the experience. You may need to obey some signs that you have not seen before, such as this one spotted near Moni Preveli in Southern Crete:

You might even have a life changing event. Nikos, from Stypsi in North Lesvos, offered to find me a wife ! Not any wife but one that would have her own olive grove. He did warn me that the size and quality of the olive grove was, however, inversely related to the attractiveness of the wife on offer. He was very proud of his own wife and his Mazda pick-up as they were similar ages and both *"still working well"*. What a character!

Profile of Sikinos *by Sylvia Cook*

An unspoilt gem, between Folegandros and Ios, **Sikinos** (Σίκινος) was the last major Cycladic island to take inter-island ferry passengers to a jetty. Just 41km² of mostly rocky terrain with some cultivated terraces in the south east, the small population lives mostly at the inland **Hora** (Χώρα), comprised of two hamlets **Horio** (Χωριό) and **Kastro** (Κάστρο), and the port of **Alopronia** (Αλοπρόνια) about 4kms away.

Alopronia has a tamarisk backed sandy beach and low key tourist facilities, whilst the Hora has cobbled streets, a few rooms, eating places, kafeneia and a free olive press museum open in high season. From Kastro you can walk to the nearby closed Zoodohou Pigis Monastery for amazing views, or take a longer walk on a new track to the Episkopi Mon-

Adapted from outline - detail from Road Editions Folegandros/Sikinos map

astery which incorporates a 3rd c AD Roman temple or mausoleum, originally thought to have been an older temple to Hera - hence its name Heroon.

Other small beaches can be visited on foot (tracks not always clear) or more easily by local caiques in season.

Sikinos Background

❏ *Known originally as Oenoe, it was the island where Thoas came ashore in a chest in which he had been put by his daughter Hypsipyle, to save him when all other men were being killed on Lemnos in revenge for their unfaithfulness with female Thracian captives.*

❏ *Settled first near the Episkopi 'Heroon' by Ionians, with little soil and no sheltered anchorage, Sikinos was not of great importance in ancient times. The Romans used it as an island for exiles.*

Stopover on Sikinos *by Gary Stevens*

In mid June a friend and I visited **Naxos** for the sixth successive year. This time we decided it was time to 'conquer' a new island as well. Taking the very ancient 'Panagia Tinou' ferry at lunchtime on a Tuesday we made the three and a half hour sea journey to the island of **Sikinos** for a one night stopover and a chance to look around.

The ferry deposited us at the port of **Alopronia** at around 5 pm. First impressions (well founded) were of a very sleepy backwater of a Greek Island, a total contrast to Naxos. A mere handful of people disembarked from the ferry and there seemed few tourists already there. The main port was blessed with just one café bar, one taverna and one mini market. After a stroll round we realised we had missed the bus to the Hora, so decided to book a room at the port straight away, in readiness for our ferry back to civilisation the next morning. There was a surprising amount of accommodation available and a number of new apartment blocks were being built too - perhaps August sees a greater influx of trade?

With only a short time to explore the island, as soon as we had deposited our bags we headed the 5 kms up the hill to **Horio** and **Kastro**. It was a very pleasant, gentle and breezy climb, passing clump after clump of wild thyme and hovering hawks. As we climbed the winding road the views back to the port and sea became more and more spectacular.

The **Hora** area also proved to be extremely quiet, untouched by mass tourism, typically and traditionally Greek in character. Kastro was full of the usual white cubist houses and similar to the unique and scenic Kastro centres also found on Folegandros, Sifnos and Kimolos.

Between Kastro and the upper part of the Hora we halted at an exposed and windswept taverna on the cliff edge with marvellous views across the sea to Folegandros. Stopping to enjoy a cool beer after the climb, we then headed back to the centre of Kastro to go to one of the two tavernas, the only one that was in fact open. The tumbler full of 'cold tea' the owner was tipping back at his table turned out to be the very palatable local wine. We enjoyed tasty traditional Greek fare here (including the wine), sitting beneath a pergola full of healthy grape vines and laden with the grapes that would be used to make next year's wine for the table.

In the morning we packed our bags and prepared for the journey back to Naxos. Having enjoyed a leisurely breakfast at the Alopronia taverna and being well on time for the ferry, as happens so often, the 'Panagia Tinou' turned up a full one and a half hours late. Well that's Greece for you !

For a truly traditional Greek island with few frills, Sikinos may be your ideal destination, or just a relaxing stopover from another island.

The Changing Face of Sikinos *by Pauline Hinson*

In 1985 we visited Sikinos when tourism was just starting. From where we were staying, on Ios, they were offering free ferry rides to Sikinos if you stayed at least two nights. It was our first trip to Greece and a chance to see another island, so we went.

There was no deep water port at Sikinos then, so we stopped in the middle of the bay and a little motor boat came to meet us. With helping hands from the ferry and the boat men, we had to jump when the boat came level with the car ramp they had lowered, as the waves bobbed us into the right position.

The man who brought the boat asked *"You want room?"* as we got to the quay. We said *"Yes"* and he told us to *"see woman"*. The woman was Flora, his wife, who ran a shop on the quay that sold everything and she ran the four rooms above. You reached the rooms by a spiral staircase outside the building. The room was very basic, two beds, two little chairs and one small wardrobe. The toilet was shared. We could see the toilet and wash basin, but no shower. With sign language we asked if there was a shower. She pointed to a box above the toilet which had a chain to pull to flush the toilet and another contraption to pull if you wanted to use it as a shower - COLD. We never bothered with that shower, but we did take the room.

Flora worked in the shop from morning to night. She was about 8 months pregnant and had two children aged about 3 and 5 hanging around her knees most of the day. Outside the shop she had a few tables where you could buy and consume beer, wine or ouzo and just sit. On the counter in the shop she had a gas stove, chip pan and frying pan. If you asked for *patatas* she would peel the potatoes and cook them in the shop, or sometimes fry *kalamares* for you. The man from the boat was Michaelis, her husband, who was also the postmaster up in the Hora.

We thought what a poor downtrodden Greek wife Flora was. There were not many tourists there at all, but it was September, so I suppose the season was winding down.

Our first night on Sikinos we decided to eat at a taverna whose lights we saw twinkling on the other side of the beach. We asked the owner for 'fish and chips' - remember, it was our first trip to Greece. He said *"big fish or little fish?"* We asked for little fish as we were not all that hungry, having eaten some chips earlier at Flora's. The smell from the kitchen was gorgeous - just like an 'English chippy'. What a shock when he brought our food to the table - two plates piled high with little fishes with their heads and tails still on. We thought he had meant 'big' or 'little' *portions* of fish. We couldn't stop laughing. His face was a picture as he watched us cut off the heads and tails and just eat the middle bit. That was our first lesson in Greece!

Next day we walked to the **Hora**. It took over an hour to get up there. The 'road' was just a dusty track, but they were starting to lay asphalt. To our amazement they had a Needham Plant Hire compressor - all the way from Stockport where we live.

There are two parts to Hora. The old part, **Horio** (village) was a shock - people were living in hovels with blankets across their doorways and the smell of goats and chickens was disgusting. We quickly walked on up to the newer part, known as **Kastro**. Looming above us was a monastery, about half a mile away, so we went for a closer look. When we got there we tried knocking on the big wooden door to see if we could look around, but there was no answer. We went around the side and heard what sounded like monks chanting and singing. After they stopped we thought we'd try the door again - still no answer. Gordon climbed over a low

wall to investigate, but returned after 10 minutes saying all was derelict and empty. There was obviously no one living there. We still can't explain the singing, but it made the hairs on the back of our necks stand on end!

Back in Kastro we found a taverna. The lady took us to show what was available. We pointed at some spaghetti and meatballs that looked very nice and went to sit outside. Less than a minute later she brought our plates of food - yes, you guessed - stone cold. Lesson number two was learnt - when ordering food in Greece ask for *'zesti'*.

We went back again twenty years on from that first trip. The harbour has been made deeper, the port is now called **Alopronia**, there is a proper road, one bus and some motor cars. Flora's is still the only shop in the harbour area, although modernised it is still open all day except for a break at siesta time. She is still lugging boxes, crates and bags of potatoes. The pregnant bump is now a twenty year old mechanic. Husband Michaelis is still the post master. Her new rooms, at The Flora Hotel, are a great improvement - 400 metres up a steep road and with wonderful sea views. Michaelis drove us up there in his car. When we got out our money to pay in advance, he said *"Give money to Flora"* which we did. Contrary to our idea of Flora as a poor downtrodden Greek wife, we now realise she is a

hard working and astute business woman.

We went up to the Hora again and had a meal in the same taverna, hot this time. Talking to a young woman related to the taverna lady, she explained that was the way everyone ate their food in those days.

One odd thing to warn you about (although perhaps it will change) there was no ticket office in the port. The agent's office is in the upper Hora and only open 9am-1pm and 5-9pm. There was only one bus every 2 hours. Considering everyone has to buy a ticket to get off the island it can cause a lot of problems - which it did for us in 2005. It seems there is much rivalry between the Hora and Alopronia port people, because the port gets more tourists. We awoke to mist on the morning of our departure, which presumably caused some of the delays, but to cut a long story short, we had to rush inland to get replacement tickets for a different boat we finally caught 9 hours later than planned.

Sikinos New Port - photo from Road Editions tourist map

It was interesting to go back after so many years and see how little Sikinos had really changed. There were more rooms to let and about 3 tavernas near Flora's shop. The same with the village, where the one shop on the main narrow street still had hardly anything on its shelves. In essence Sikinos is still one of Greece's remaining sleepy unspoilt islands.

How to get to Sikinos
By Air - Scheduled or charter flights to Athens, Santorini
By Ferry - From Piraeus or Lavrion on mainland, links with most Cyclades
Package Tour Operators - Greek Sun, Hidden Greece, Island Wandering.

What Shall We Do Today?

Our Usual Lazy Rhythm *by Tony Davis*

Naxos was as captivating as ever and our time there mostly indolent as usual. Major decision of the day: lunch *in* Paradisos Taverna or under the 2 little tamarisks *outside*? Is the music inside good today? (Nearly always is.) Is it too windy outside today? Are all the shaded tables taken?

Either way - what shall we eat? Which of the 30 (yes, 30) possibilities to choose? All of them are superb with fresh vegetables grown on the taverna owner's farm; the service is good, the whole place big enough for 250 people, but efficiently organised, completely informal and friendly, with frequent freebies of ices, coffee, etc, etc.

Outside, the view never fails to transfix me: Paros to the west, rocks to the south, coast of Naxos to the southeast with isthmus, low lying, leading out to a pyramidal headland from which rocks sprinkle outwards. How far will we see today? On a clear day Ios and Sikinos are visible. On a *very* clear day Folegandros and the southern tip of Antiparos too !

Shall we walk, to and from, 'splishy splashy' along the cooling water's edge, or through the trees and shrubbery along sandy paths, past the man (usually snoozing) with the tethered donkey?

Decisions, decisions! Oh the agony of it all.

Rude Awakening *by Tony Davis*

My post prandial snooze was interrupted, *"Mister, mister"* in a male Greek voice, *"You must put on your trunks."* Trunks, what trunks? This was one of the generally accepted nudist beach areas of the Greek islands, but two Greek cops loomed up.

Then to Lorraine *"Lady, pleased to get cloth-ed".* All around us people were

reluctantly covering up. As we rummaged for clothes the cops moved on.

After a while there was a great commotion from farther along the beach: cheering; a Greek woman's voice, high pitched and angry; more cheering - and clapping. The concerto continued: vigorous soloist and a strongly assertive orchestra. I ran over to where a crowd had gathered and was giving great vocal support to a young Greek woman, scantily clothed, haranguing the two abashed and totally dumbfounded officers of the law.

According to a subsequent translation her gist was:

"Why must we cover our bodies? God made our bodies. They are beautiful. We are not ashamed of the bodies the good God gives us" ... all egged on by the crowd clapping, cheering, laughing ... *"Why do you make us angry? Why don't you arrest the men who hide in the bushes and look at us and masturbate? ..."*

The policemen silently left the scene !

Along Came a Spider *by Pauline Hinson*

Most beaches on Leros are pebbly, but one day we climbed over some rocks and found a little beach with rather more sand, so we settled down on our towels for some *heliotherapy*. From over the rocks a man and his son appeared with rakes and started clearing the beach, throwing rocks and large stones to the back to expose more sand. He did say not to bother moving, but we did, to allow them to finish the job.

Shortly after I was relaxing, laid on my back, when I felt something tickle my leg. I sat up and saw it was a brown spider, about one inch long. As I am arachnophobic I shot to my feet like a rocket, shaking my towel and dancing about. Panic over, I settled back down, but 15 minutes later I felt a sting on my left knee and was horrified to see the spider back again. I screamed. Gordon (normally an animal and spider lover) got a stone and battered it to death in case it was a poisonous one. I panicked a bit as there was a spot of blood on my knee and it was really stinging, but I applied my trusty 'after-bite' stick and it didn't swell up.

Reassured, I relaxed again and mused that it had probably been living happily under one of the stones that had been cleared, before we had invaded its territory.

A little while later a big ant appeared on my beach towel, dragging the crumpled body of the poor dead spider behind it. I just sat transfixed as the ant struggled, first dragging, then moving around to push the spider from behind, across my towel and then the sand, presumably to a spot where he would be able to enjoy the feast.

Koufonisi Idyll *by Hilary Ludbrook*

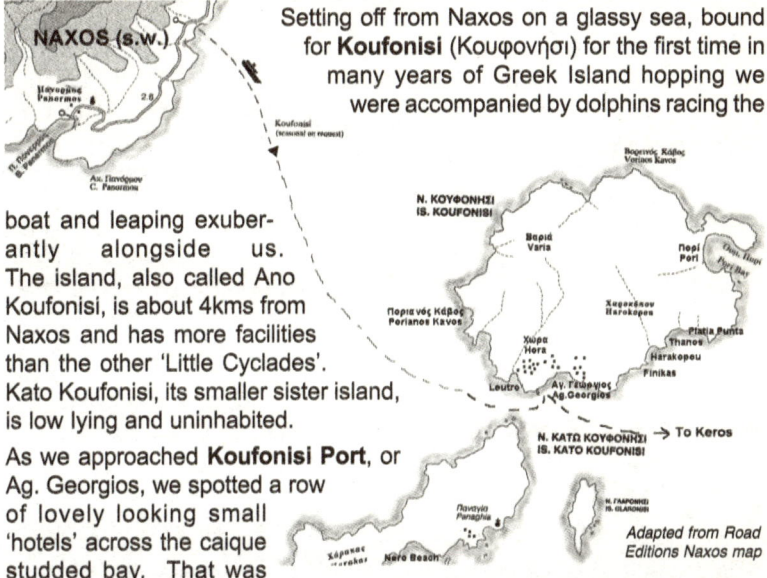

Setting off from Naxos on a glassy sea, bound for **Koufonisi** (Κουφονήσι) for the first time in many years of Greek Island hopping we were accompanied by dolphins racing the

boat and leaping exuberantly alongside us. The island, also called Ano Koufonisi, is about 4kms from Naxos and has more facilities than the other 'Little Cyclades'. Kato Koufonisi, its smaller sister island, is low lying and uninhabited.

As we approached **Koufonisi Port**, or Ag. Georgios, we spotted a row of lovely looking small 'hotels' across the caique studded bay. That was

Adapted from Road Editions Naxos map

where we wanted to stay. There was the usual kerfuffle of islanders with rooms to let mobbing the disembarking visitors, but we hung back wanting to do our own recce. Eventually we made our way across the sand track and were accosted by a young lady from the Maria Rooms - just the building we fancied most. Unfortunately they were just rooms and not studios, but we fell in love with the view and Maria promised she would provide a Gaz stove for the sad English people who needed 24 hour access to a cuppa!

We unpacked and admired the harbour view for as long as we could - but no sign of our stove, so eventually we went in search of Maria. After a lot of nervous peering around in private areas, I tracked her down in her mother's kitchen. A lot of sign language eventually produced mum's own stove, but no offer of anything to boil the water *in*. More arm waving and mum dug out one of those long-handled coffee 'briki' things from the depths of her cupboard. Success! We enjoyed our long anticipated drink from our own mugs (which we always bring) and relaxed at last.

As the sun set we turned our thoughts to showers before going out for food. The shower room was all brand new, but tiny. Only now did we realise that to sit on the loo you had to have your feet in the shower tray and that the loo roll holder was on the shower wall so we had soggy loo paper ... typical Greek planning ! Next came the challenge of plugging in the pretty lamp

provided. We eventually found the socket down by the side of the ward-robe. The only way to have the lamp on was to trail the cable in front of the wardrobes - so every time we wanted clothes in or out we had to unplug the lamp. No matter, we still loved it - until breakfast next morning when the gas ran out. Our next door neighbours came to our rescue. They had brought their own gas stove, frying pan, etc and let us have their spare cylinder with instructions as to where we could buy a replacement.

This turned out to be a dark, scary 'Aladdin's Cave' of a shop at the back of the beach (fans of The League of Gentlemen  will understand if I say it was 'a local shop for local people'). Some things here were very cheap and some unexpectedly very expensive, as we real-ised when we discovered the brand new and huge - by Greek standards - supermarket at the top of the hill on the way to **Hora**. There were at least two other shops on this tiny island, although it is no more than 3 kms across. I've no idea how they could all make a living.

We walked along the coastal path which connects the beautiful beaches along the south eastern side of the island. It's only 10 minutes to the first beach which has a taverna, but we carried on to one with several nooks and cran-nies to tuck ourselves into. The water was unbelievably clear. Later we walked along to **Pori** (Πορί) the last and largest beach. My husband couldn't resist a swim in the 30-foot deep rock water hole we passed. Pori has a beautiful sweep of fine, white sand with incredibly turquoise water which you just can't dive into quickly enough. In September there were only a handful of others there - mostly 'au naturel'. The only thing to spoil it was the not uncom-mon almost-built taverna at the back of the beach, complete with rubble heaps that seemed compulsory on every island we visited in our 5 week holiday.

We tried several tavernas during our 3-night stay and did not see a menu in any of them. We find it a bit unnerving not knowing in advance how much things cost, but it was all fairly cheap. The only disappointment was at Nicholas Taverna which had been recommended in guide books, but things can change and we found the service very poor and unfriendly, the food indifferent. My chicken souvlaki was a frozen 'fast food' reconstituted ver-sion and stone cold. We know the Greeks like their food luke warm and can usually cope with this, but this was a step too far and we had to ask for it to be reheated. It was also the most expensive meal of our whole trip.

On our way back to our room we stopped at a very attractive stone-built bar at the top of the village. It had a lively atmosphere - all Greeks, candle lit and very romantic with several cosy alcoves to snuggle into. We settled down with our ouzos and my husband put his arm around me as we discussed our favourite times and places on the islands.

Suddenly he whispered to me *"Your bottom's vibrating!"* *"...What do you mean?"* *"It's vibrating ..."* he moved his arm and we turned to look behind.

There was a tiny mouse, trying to burrow into my fleece! Naturally I leapt up, but the mouse was unconcerned and began tucking into a stray peanut without a care in the world. Our mirth attracted the other customers and mayhem broke out. One chap arrived brandishing his bar stool in lion-taming fashion. The bar owner was obviously concerned that the mouse shouldn't get into his kitchen, so there was general panic, shouting and gesticulating. We left them to it and retired to the calm of our balcony to watch the moon over the water.

The next day we went again to Pori, but this time we walked back along the middle to the west side of the island. At least that was the plan. We had Dieter Graf's 'Walking the Aegean Islands' book with photographs showing every stage of the walk, which had seemed such a good idea until you realise that every mule track and whitewashed church look the same - and if you are lost you're not going to see that particular view anyway !

Eventually we struggled around the southwestern corner of the island and stumbled on another harbour - absolutely full to bursting with fishing caiques and all manner of small boats. The wind had picked up and it had clouded over, but it wasn't until the main port came into view that we realised that ALL the boats had been taken to the little enclosed harbour for safety. Mikaelis, our room owner, was racing round raising the awnings on all the balconies and predicting a force seven gale. We had already experienced long delays and detours due to gales and were planning to leave the next day. However, things weren't as bad as expected and the next day was calm again - but the bay looked quite naked without its colourful fishing fleet as we ferried away from our idyllic little island.

How to get to Koufonisi

By Air - Scheduled or charter flights to Athens or Mykonos - then ferry

By Ferry - closest is Naxos, also connected with Amorgos, Donoussa, Heraklia, Kea, Kythnos, Lavrio, Paros, Piraeus, Schinoussa, Syros.

Package Tour Operators - Greek Sun, Hidden Greece, Island Wandering.

The Farthest Greek Shore *by Don Henderson*

It was in 1991, a long time ago, but, we think, still a tale worth telling ! We should have known better I suppose, but we planned, actually planned in some detail, a two-venue holiday in the Dodecanese. First a week in **Kastelorizo** (Καστελοριζο), or **Megisti** (Μεγίστι) to the Greeks, by ferry from Rhodes, followed by a week in our 'second home' in **Karpathos**, which, with connections via Rhodes, worked out to three weeks away from home.

Kastelorizo Position & detail

Adapted from
Road Editions
All Greece map

As regular visitors to 'off the beaten track' Karpathos, we had often wondered how Kastelorizo, about 70 nautical miles east of Rhodes, would compare. It's so far-flung from the rest of its country, it is often left off maps of Greece.

Our planning included booking by post (website bookings were yet to catch on) a pension in the **old town** of **Rhodes**, so that, on arrival at 3.30 in the morning, beds would be waiting for us to rest before our onward journey. In the event, the place was deserted, 'they' having decided that our arrival was at 3.30pm. My wife just could not stand any longer, so she laid on the tiled floor of the pension reception area and tried to sleep, while I watched the dawn come up behind a Greek windmill - picturesque, but a bit wearing. Not a very good start, but worse was to follow, for when we went to take the weekly ferry to K2, as we called Kastelorizo (Karpathos being our K1), we were told that it had broken down at Patmos, and no-one knew when it would arrive. Action was called for, so we rebooked, and caught another ferry to Karpathos, arriving at 4.30am, to spend a hectic, but pleasant holiday with our friends.

Our ferry back to Rhodes on a Saturday, neatly avoided the K2 ferry, if it ran. Planes to K2 being small and few and far between, we were surprised to be able to book on Monday for a Tuesday flight to Kastelorizo. After we checked in at the airport our flight never appeared on the departure board, but was well filled when we were finally on our way. The journey was made more

pleasant by a Greek gentleman with excellent English, sitting next to my wife, who told us a lot about the island and said expatriates were returning for a celebration, which presumably explained the extra flights.

The island was incredible. Absolutely idyllic for us - not so much for what it had, but for what it hadn't got ! No buses, no taxis, a minibus from the airport seeming to be the only ordinary transport on the island. The scenery was beautiful, particularly the enormous deep harbour, which had been filled with great ships in the days of sail. Shops were very limited. In fact, when I broke my sandal strap, there was neither a cobbler, nor a shop that sold shoes, so I had to live for our stay in a pair of flip-flops (which I hate), purchased from the periptero. It seemed that even a haircut would have meant a trip to Rhodes, as there were no commercial ferry boats to Turkey just a few kilometres away at the closest point. No surprise that, as relations were not good at that time. Small boats came over from Turkey, however, stayed an hour or two, and then went back. Tourists we wondered ?

The ruined red stone Venetian castle (Castello Rosso) on a hill behind the main harbour gave the island its modern name and commanded views over the harbour and bays either side, and the streets and buildings of what had been a much larger town below. The island suffered heavily during the war, and the original town was still in ruins with no rebuilding here. We were told that the population was evacuated during the war, but that the ship bringing back the returnees sank, and many lives were lost.

A new village was being constructed nearby, presumably to replace the bombed area, and the workmen filled the few pensions, some of them sharing ours (very muddy!). A long walk down one side of the harbour took one to the only Hotel, with access to the harbour for swimming - a wonderful experience. There must have been fifty feet depth of clear water, with fish

galore swimming about. It was well worth the walk.

On Friday 13th (believe it or not) we were up early, but had to rush to join the whole population at the **Hora**, for a packed service in the Cathedral. To our astonishment, our friend from the plane, Mr K. as we called him, gave the main address, and was obviously an important dignitary. A Greek warship had arrived at the quay, and a helicopter flew in with more dignitaries.

At the end of the service, everyone processed down a winding road, to the quayside where a memorial stood. For what seemed an age, wreath after wreath was laid with due ceremony. It was clearly quite an occasion. Soldiers, sailors, dignitaries, and the whole population gathered for 'Independence Day'. Very impressive, colourful, and obviously a real community event. The afternoon was spent in a quayside taverna, watching the helicopter and the warship depart, while the place returned to normal.

The rest of the holiday was restful, the only other event being a trip to the Blue Cave, in a blow-up dinghy. It was very beautiful. As far as we could tell we were the only non-Greek tourists on the island, but we made some friends among the ex-pats, some of whom seemed to come back every year from as far away as Australia.

Some years later, we heard that an Italian film had been made on Kastelorizo, called 'Mediterraneo', which we obtained as a video and enjoy greatly from time to time. It is a lovely story of a stranded Italian Army unit and their relationships with the locals. As a result of this, we were told, a number of Italians decided to follow in the film crew's footsteps and visit the island, so Kastelorizo has been opened up somewhat.

With a few more ferries in season and even a catamaran service, we understand that it has become a favourite destination amongst wealthy Greeks and international jet setters who escape to its pretty village to relax, eat and drink at fish tavernas set around the deep harbour, swim in the clear water made accessible from ladders set in the side, go snorkelling, walking or for boat trips. There are no real beaches, apart from one very small area by the new village houses, but it is still a perfect island for relaxation.

Unfortunately, we are no longer able to make what would be a most interesting return visit to our unforgettable holiday isle on Greece's farthest shore !

How to get to Kastelorizo
By Air - Scheduled or domestic flights via Rhodes
By Ferry - From/to Rhodes only
Package Tour Operators - Greek Sun, Hidden Greece, Island Wandering.

Profile of Zakynthos *by Sylvia Cook*

South of Kefalonia and west of the Peloponnese, the Ionian Island of Zakynthos (Ζάκυνθος) is 400 km² of mountains (rising to 756m), fertile plains and farming villages, wooded hills and valleys, and coastal resorts in the east and southeast with some of the best sandy beaches in Greece. Also known by its Venetian name of Zante, it was dubbed the 'Venice' or 'Flower of the East'.

Although tourism is well developed and accessible from many regional UK airports making it a popular destination for the British, there are still unspoilt villages and traditional rural areas, plus smaller newly developed resorts.

Map labels:

Cape Skinari
Κορίθι / Korithi
Blue Cave
Ελιές / Elies
Βολίμες / Volimes 14
12
Ασκός / Askos
Ag.Nikolaos
Navagio B. Shipwreck
Σκινάρια / Skinaria
Ορθονιές / Orthonies
Αγ. Γεωργίου / Agh. Georgiou
Αναφωνήτρια / Anafonitria
Κατασταρι / Katastari 21
Αλυκές / Alykes
Αλικανάς / Alikanas
Αλώνια / Alonia
Πόρτο / Porto Βρομή / Vromi
Μαριές / Maries
Καλλιθέα / Kalithea
Γερακάρι / Gerakari
Κypseli
Planos
Tsilivi Bay
Έξω Χώρα / Exo Hora 27
Σκουληκάδο / Skoulikado
Τραγάκι / Tragaki
Ακρωτήρι / Akrotiri
Αγ. Κήρυκος / Agh. Kirykos
Βανάτο / Vanato
Μπόχαλη / Bochali
Zakynthos / Ζάκυνθος
Καμπί / Kambi
Op. Βραχίωνας / Mt. Vrachionas
Αγ. Λέων / Agh. Leon
Μαχαιράδο / Macherado 10
Αργάσι / Argasi
Κοιλιόμενο / Kiliomeno
4
Αμπελόκηποι / Ambelokipi
10
14
Ξηροκάστελο / Xirokastelo
Παντοκράτορας / Pandokrataras
Λαγανάς / Laganas
Αιθάκια / Lithakia
Καλαμάκι / Kalamaki
Βασιλικός / Vasilikos
Αγαλάς / Agalas
11
Ag.Sostis
Gerakas
Π. Κερί / B. Keri
Κερί / Keri

Inset map:
Preveza
CENTRAL GREECE
Lefkada (Lefkas)
IONIAN SEA
Meganissi
Ithaka
Kefalonia
Kilini
Zakynthos (Zante)
PELOPONNESE

Adapted from Road Editions Road Atlas, Zakynthos & Ionian Maps available

Zakynthos Background

☐ *Called Zakynthos since Homer's time, it was an important trade centre, at times allied to Athens and Sparta, taken by Macedonians, then Romans, unprotected during Byzantine years, then given to the Franks in 1204. The Venetian occupation 1489 -1797 probably had the greatest influence on modern day Zante. The French ruled briefly, then it was a British protectorate with other Ionians until Greek reunification in 1864.*

☐ *Natural 'pitch' from springs at Keri was used to waterproof ships' hulls since ancient times (mentioned by Herodotus) - now less productive.*

- Zakynthian poet, Dionysius Solomos (1798-1857), wrote the Greek National anthem lyrics 'Hymn to Freedom', and was one of the first renowned poets to write in demotic Greek.

- The island suffered extensive damage in the 1953 earthquakes. The main town was rebuilt based on the old Venetian plan, only a few Venetian buildings survived.

Zante - My Summer Retreat *by Bill Harper*

"Yassoo Billy"

"Yassoo Billy moo"

The welcoming greetings can be heard from all parts of the **Kypseli** (Κυψέλη) kafeneion as I approach. Although 'kafeneion' strictly means 'coffee house' it far more frequently sells beer and ouzo - as well as miscellaneous commonly needed general stores.

"Yassas" I answer, waving my arm languidly - 'languidly' because that is the only way the elderly patrons do things here, since for most of them anything more energetic might easily precipitate a heart attack.

I order an ouzo with ice - well, to be more exact, I do if Spiros isn't there, because if he is he'll order for me and pay as well. Spiros and I battle throughout my stay on Zante playing a kind of game of Snap - only in our game whoever sees the other first shouts *"Ouzo!"* and then under the rules he is allowed to buy the loser a glass of the Greek aniseed spirit. But it's not easy for me to win since Spiros is more often than not inhabiting a dark corner of the shop and sees me approaching before I am even aware of him. But I do win if I am at the shop first and seated outside (I don't go to Greece to sit in dark corners) and if I see him clambering out of his battered old van with his back to me.

Actually it is very difficult to buy a Greek a drink in Greece. He takes the view that as a visitor to his country you are his guest and it's his delight to extend every courtesy to you (except when driving on the road!). Although Spiros comes from Kypseli, he doesn't live here now, but comes from the main town some six miles south where he runs a taverna that doesn't have written menus. Instead customers gather at around 9.30 to 10 o'clock in the evening (Greek evenings don't start until at least 9.00pm) whereupon the manageress goes from table to table verbally reciting today's menu and taking orders. Then, surprisingly quickly, the food appears - as does a small band who walk amongst the customers regaling them with Greek songs both sentimental and bawdy - in the traditional Ionian kantades style.

Sat relaxed on the coffee shop balcony I dreamily survey the part of the village that spreads below me. First the short narrow village street with trees and houses interspersed along its length, then a view down a long gentle tree-covered slope to the wide expanse of the Ionian Sea. Looking a little to my right I am able to see the misty coast of the Peloponnese, whilst to my left I can see the towering mountain on Kefalonia, so near that it seems to be a part of Zakynthos itself. Indeed Captain Corelli would be within spitting distance of where I sit, could I but spit over a low mountain and seven miles of sea.

Zakynthos (which the Venetians named Zante) is a 'just right' size of island - some 25 miles by 12, mountains in the west and north, beaches in the south (which tourists dispute with loggerhead turtles) and a ridge of hills on the east below which more beaches can be found. It has all you need within reasonable reach, without being too squeezed in. Also, unusually for a Greek island, it has a lush central lowland that from above always reminds me of Tolkien's Shire, lying between the hills of the east and the mountains of the west and north.

Spring Views - from Simpson Travel brochure

But I rarely go up into the mountain. Nothing to do there. Mind you, there's nothing much to do in Kypseli - but it's a different kind of nothing.

Kypseli is perched on one of the eastern hills. Greek 'coastal' villages are often built on inland hills because in earlier times they were less visible from passing pirate ships. It is a dying village. The youngsters have gone off to work and live in more eventful places. Yet it is also a growing village since houses are being built all around - either to replace previous older small houses, or as new 'holiday homes' in a place where the owners have family roots. Incidentally, a typical house here is somewhat better than a typical house in most of England. As someone once commented, Greece may be a poor country, but the Greeks have plenty of money! Mind you, as well as money the Greeks have innate DIY skills and cheap Albanian labour to help them build their houses.

I visit Kypseli every year now, but most tourists are taken to coastal resorts

where life can be very different, so here are a few thoughts that may help new visitors enjoy their Zakynthos experience.

The main tourist resorts in descending order of 'lager-loutishness' are **Laganas** (Λαγανάς) - best avoided by Grecophiles - **Argasi** (Αργάσι), **Tsilivi** (Τσιλιβή), **Alikes** (Αλυκές), **Alikanas** (Αλυκανάς). Smaller resorts more recently developed for tourists are **Kalamaki** (Καλαμάκι) and **Ag. Sostis** (Αγ. Σώστις), both really extensions to Laganas; **Vasilikos** (Βασιλικός) and **Gerakas** (Γέρακας) in the south east have beaches such as Porto Zoro and Amouthia; **Limni Keri** (Λίμνη Κερί), developed near a nature reserve and traditional village on the southern tip, is fairly laid back; **Ag. Nikolaos** (Αγ. Νικόλαος) in the far north is worth finding, although rarely in brochures.

Limni Keri - from Sunvii brochure

Generally the 'better' part of the island is north of the city of Zakynthos where most of the traditional Greek village settlements are (visit hill villages **Kypseli, Tragaki** (Τραγάκι), **Ano Gerakari** (Ανω Γερακάρι), but the Argasi to Vasilikos peninsula is probably the more visually attractive area.

The island has wonderful sandy beaches on the eastern coast and at the head and east of Laganas Bay in the south, but the latter beaches are shared with endangered loggerhead turtles, so best left empty outside resort areas.

The mountains have little spectacular to see, although there is some eye-catching cliff scenery at **Kambi** (Καμπί) - the local execution ground in the Civil War of the 1940's. You don't need much imagination to work out how they were executed. **Volimes** (Βολίμες) high in the northwest is a centre for local lace-work and carpets.

There is little to see on Zakynthos, except the coast from a boat trip around the island or a shorter trip to the **Blue Caves** (Γαλάζια Σπήλαια) in the north near Cape Skinari - blue because the light enters under water, so as a result of refraction swirls and drops have a bluish tinge. The most famous sight, on many posters, is the deserted wreck - an early 20th century rusty steam boat - but getting to see it involves a long trip over the mountains to **Porto Vromi** (Ο.Βρώμη) or the boat trip. To see the wreck from above, there is a viewing platform on top of the cliffs, accessed after passing through **Anafonitria** (Αναφωνήτρια). Ask in the village which road to take.

With **Kilini** (Κυλήνη) in the Peloponnese just one hour away by frequent ferry, a trip to **Olympia**, home of the ancient Olympic games, can easily be completed in a day - a good opportunity if you have not been there before.

Parking in **Zakynthos Town** in the tourist season can be horrendous and The National Bank of Greece is always the most crowded, to be avoided if possible. It is a working town, but there are hotels, restaurants and bars as well as the port and bus station if you want to base yourself here. You may like to visit the ruined Venetian kastro behind the town (believed to have collapsed in the 1515 earthquake), or wander round the back streets of small shops, mostly open only during Greek business hours.

For me the best all-round restaurant on the island is the one next to the church on the very top of the hill at **Ano Gerakari** - great views too. Another popular restaurant with Greeks (ie most authentic Greek cooking) but also English speaking is Plantinos in **Vanato** (Βανάτο), 5 km west of the main town, although it is just a low cost family run grill-restaurant. If you do go, tell Andreas you heard about him from me.

Zante is surprisingly green considering where it is, although the west side of Greece does receive more rain than other parts. Indeed I've never been aware of any water shortage despite day after day of cloudless blue skies in the summer. Yet at other times of the year it can be as cold, wet and miserable as a stereotypical Manchester day. A few years back a UK TV series about four British women married to Zakynthians was entitled *Island of Dreams* - and so it is, in the summer.

An increasingly loud drone approaching tells me an aircraft is ferrying another load of passengers back home.

"Oh, what," I ask myself, *"can those Englanders fly to, which is half as precious as that they fly from?"* (With apologies to someone or other.)

How to get to Zakynthos

By Air - Scheduled via Athens or direct charter from most regional UK airports (Birmingham, Bristol, Cardiff, East Midlands, Edinburgh, Gatwick, Glasgow, Humberside, Luton, Manchester, Newcastle, Nottingham, Stanstead)

By Ferry - from/to Kilini in NW Peloponnese, links with Kefalonia.

Package Tour Operators - Most mainstream, plus Greek specialists: Amathus, Argo, Best of Greece, Direct Greece, Elysian, Greek Options, Island Wandering, Kosmar, Manos, Olympic Holidays, Planet, Simply Travel, Simpson Travel, Solos, Sunisle, Sunvil.

Big Mother is Watching You *by Bill Harper*

Although the Greeks are quite happy to let you do as you wish and leave you alone when you visit, they are nevertheless watching in case you run into trouble. One evening whilst in Zakynthos, I misjudged the position of my car when negotiating a tight bend and my front right-hand wheel slid into the roadside ditch. I put the car into reverse, but to my dismay this failed to bring the wheel back onto the road. Yet before I could even get out to assess matters, I was surrounded by half a dozen excited Greeks carrying ropes and directing a car behind me into position. Within a couple of minutes this other car had pulled me out of the ditch.

How many other places in Western Europe (or even the World) could one slide into a ditch and be pulled out by perfect strangers in less than five minutes? Nor was this a one-off. Two years ago my clutch totally failed in a remote mountain district on the mainland where not a soul nor house was in sight. It was a Saturday, midday on a bank holiday weekend, yet four hours later after a seven-mile tow, I was on my way again - for a cost that was no more than some garages in England would have charged for the tow alone.

I doubt if many visitors who leave the tourist enclaves to drive around the countryside are aware of the all-encompassing supportive net that the locals weave around them. Eyes follow them virtually all the time. Not the eyes of Big Brother and CCTV, but the caring eyes of Big Mother leaving them unaware of any attention, until something goes wrong.

Stop in a remote mountain lay-by and you may notice some passing cars moving strangely slowly - just checking! Lift the bonnet to dip-check the oil and a passing car will pull in the same lay-by, seemingly to admire the view, but then quickly drive off if all seems OK - just checking! Go for a walk and not be back before dark and some car will pass you at a crawl and maybe offer a lift - just checking!

Tourists are all too often unaware of this net until they run into trouble. Then they congratulate themselves on their good fortune at finding such helpful people at hand. Coincidence? - my foot!

Vonitsa - A Greek Seaside Town *by Pat Fitton*

In 1983 on our first trip to Greece we visited **Vonitsa** (Βόνιτσα) in the west of the mainland region of Aitoloakarnania. In September 2006 we went back, to see if Vonitsa had changed from the traditional seaside town catering for Greek visitors, which we remembered with such pleasure.

Vonitsa is situated on the south side of the **Amvrakikos Gulf** (Αμβράκικος Κόλπος), about 20 minutes drive from Preveza airport. The Vonitsa-Preveza bus passes the airport entrance and will stop on request, but services are infrequent, so we took a taxi for just €10.

Our first surprise was the journey through the new road tunnel *under* the Gulf, replacing the former ferry service across the straits - much quicker and more convenient. The town of Vonitsa is situated on a large bay, with a Venetian castle on a hill to one side, and a small church on an island towards the other side. There are two small fishing harbours near the church.

We stayed at the Hotel Vonitsa, right in the middle of the promenade, with sea-facing balcony from which we watched glorious sunsets and the evening *volta* - the gentle stroll of local inhabitants and visitors along the promenade, showing off new babies, meeting one another and stopping to exchange greetings and to chat. Our double room cost us €40 per night and breakfast was extra, however, the full size fridge in the room was a bonus as we could keep drinks, fruit, yogourt, etc cool for picnics or balcony snacks. The hotel is clean and comfortable, with spacious public areas and a sea-facing terrace on the ground floor and the staff were friendly and helpful. Swimming was excellent from a long pebble beach, which shelves quite quickly.

First impressions were that Vonitsa had not changed fundamentally. The promenade was still uncluttered by tourist tat shops. The Venetian castle, once mostly inaccessible beneath thick vegetation, was well on the way to restoration. The shingle causeway to the church on the island had been replaced with a pedestrian bridge which was illuminated after dark. A small yacht marina had been built at the foot of the castle, the source of most of the (few) foreign visitors. The traditional restaurants were still there, although more had appeared along with some café-bars towards the marina end. The town has inevitably expanded on the edges, but it remains a traditional Greek country town, with proper town shops including agricultural tool and feed stores.

A bus took us to nearby **Preveza** (Πρέβεζα), a larger but also very traditional port town on the northern tip of the Amvrakikos Gulf. We stayed overnight here to give us a full day to visit the huge site of ancient **Nikopolis**, just a short taxi ride out of town. At the far end of the Preveza promenade you can look out over the narrow straits towards **Actium** (Άκτιον) where the battle of the same name between the fleet of Mark Antony and Cleopatra and that of Octavian took place in 31 BC. As a result of his victory, Octavian confirmed himself as Emperor of Rome. (He later took the name Augustus). The city of Nikopolis was founded to commemorate his victory, and to secure military control over western Greece. It was originally populated by forcible removals from neighbouring villages and towns.

Exploring Preveza itself was enjoyable. The Venetian castle of Agios Andreas is in the centre of town. Among several churches of interest is the cathedral of Agios Haralambous, with its carved and gilded iconostasis, in the heart of the old town next to the landmark Venetian clock tower.

On Saturday night the quayside and promenade were throbbing with life - families, youngsters, visitors, a church service being broadcast over loudspeakers and a KKE (Communist Party) meeting on the quay, plus traditional Greek music competing with rap and pop. The restaurants were full of Greek families in the evenings, but there were some foreign tourists too, mostly berthed at the large yacht marina.

We also travelled by bus to the island of **Lefkada** (Λευκάδα) along the causeway and bridge from the mainland (just 20 minutes away). There was plenty of time to explore the narrow Italianate alleys and Romanesque churches with their separate bell towers in Lefkada Town and the fortress of **Santa Mavra** (Σάντα Μάυρα) on the mainland side of the causeway. On Tuesdays there is a large market in Lefkada town, and there are lots of traditional food shops with local delicacies as well as the usual tourist outlets. Despite the growth of marinas, there is still good bird watching to be had on the lagoons.

In Vonitsa our favourite restaurant was the nearest to the Hotel Vonitsa, the last in that direction going towards the island church, with tables out onto the beach, and simply called Estiatorio (Εστιατόριο). All the other restaurants we visited also served good traditional Greek food, catering for an almost entirely Greek clientele.

Vonitsa is well connected with long distance bus services - south to **Amfilochia** (Αμφιλοχία), **Agrinio** (Αγρίνιο) and **Athens** (Αθήνα) and north to **Arta** (Άρτα) and **Ioanina** (Ιωάνινα).

In spite of good intentions to explore further afield, we were lulled into swimming, walks around the castle and to the island church, and long lazy lunches.

The hotel we had stayed at in 1983 had since been turned into a police station, and we often watched as regular sorties were made from there at lunchtime to the other end of town to crack down on parking violations. Ten minutes of frantic whistle blowing, shouting and gesticulating resulted in one or two cars being moved a fraction. Honour satisfied, the police went away, presumably to lunch, and the cars were soon back in their original places.

Late on the warm evenings the older folk came to sit on the jetties and enjoy a chat. On our last evening one lady joined us on a bench, smiled and simply said *"oraya"* (ωραία - beautiful, lovely). What more was there to say?

Profile of Aegina *by Fiona Collingwood*

Aegina (Άιγινα), sometimes spelt Eyina or Egina, situated in the middle of the Saronic Gulf, has a population of 13,500 (2002) and area of 85 km². The highest peak of this hilly, fertile, triangular shaped island is Mount Oros at 532 metres.

It is popular with Athenians as a week-end retreat, lying just 20 kilometres south-west of Piraeus - a short hop by ferry (1.5 hrs) or Flying Dolphin (45 mins) to **Aegina Town**, or **Souvala** (Σουβάλα) or **Ag. Marina** (Αγ.Μαρίνα) ports. The **temple of Aphaia**'s 24 surviving Doric columns (of the original 34 in 5th c BC) are its most famous sight, but Aegina Town's single column from a **temple of Apollo** is older, from 6th c BC.

Aegina Background

☐ *Believed to have been occupied since Neolithic times, around 1000 BC the island emerged as a powerful commercial centre. In 7th cBC it produced the first coinage of the western world, made of silver and showing a turtle.*

from www. fleur-de-coin.com

☐ *The island is named from the myth of Aegina, the daughter of Assopas (a river God), whom Zeus fell in love with and carried off to an island in the Saronic gulf. She gave birth to a boy, Aeacus who became the king of the island.*

☐ *The island's golden years were in the 1820's when it became the capital of modern Greece under Ioannis Kapodistrias, albeit for not much more than a year 1826-28. The military academy, the national printing press and the National Bank were founded and the first currency of the new country was minted here - the first modern drachma coin showed a Phoenix rising from the ashes.*

☐ *Pistachio nuts were introduced just 90 years ago. Now there are 200,000 trees and the annual production is 1300 tons, but they take a heavy toll on water supplies. (See p131 for health properties of pistachios.)*

☐ *Many artists and intellectuals have lived on Aegina including Varnalis, Kazantzakis (he wrote Zorba the Greek and served as a minister in the Greek government whilst here), Seferis, Elytis and Capralos (see sculpture museum on Aegina).*

Aegina - Our Special Island *by Fiona Collingwood*

We visit Aegina as often as we can. It is like a home from home for us and holds many special memories. It was often a haven for a few hours on a day trip when we lived in busy Athens and needed a break from city life.

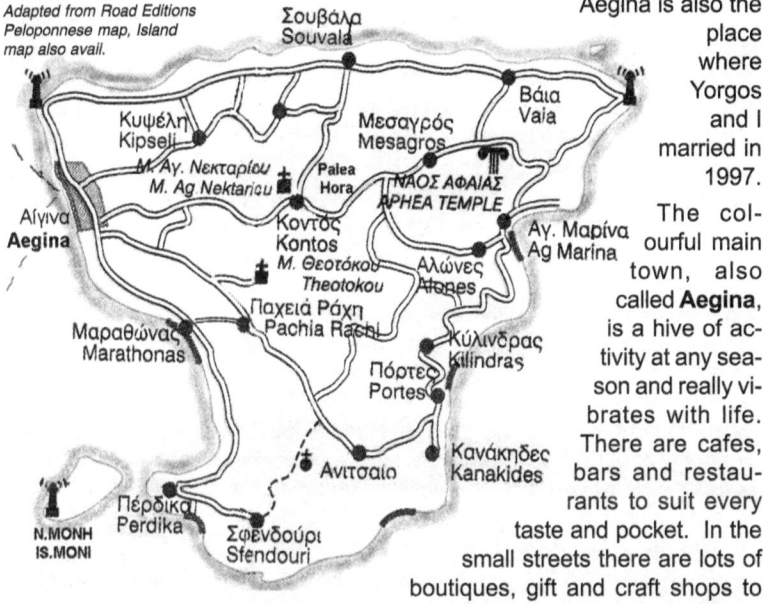

Adapted from Road Editions Peloponnese map, Island map also avail.

Aegina is also the place where Yorgos and I married in 1997.

The colourful main town, also called **Aegina**, is a hive of activity at any season and really vibrates with life. There are cafes, bars and restaurants to suit every taste and pocket. In the small streets there are lots of boutiques, gift and craft shops to wander around. Despite being a magnet for tourists and increasingly attractive to foreigners who want to make a second home in Greece, it has not lost its Greek charm and ranks highly for us in our list of favourite islands.

Our wedding was to be held in the Panayitsa church at the end of the seafront in the main town, but first I had to be baptised into the Greek Orthodox church. This was organised at our local church in Athens - the easiest part. The paperwork we needed to get married required a lot of legwork and hours waiting in queues, in church offices, around Athens and in England. Nothing went smoothly - the town hall in **Hydra** (responsible for Aegina's administration) lost my birth certificate so we had to arrange another copy from the UK.

Eventually the big day arrived. My family and a few British friends had flown out to join us with Yorgos' immediate family and close friends. We wanted to keep the occasion small and not have a 'Big' Greek wedding. I had been to a few that had been loud and chaotic. In Greece the congregation do not need to sit down, they are free to stand and move around the church, to pop

in and out, often for a smoke! It is not a solemn silent affair and can be quite noisy. I liked the informality, but did not want the noise levels.

The forty-five minute service was memorable. My father took me to the top of the church steps where Yorgos was waiting with the priest, who linked our hands and led us into the church, with our guests following behind. Inside the church the smell of incense filled the air and the building glowed from the light cast by huge golden chandeliers. At the altar were two *lambathes* (candles) about a metre and a half high, decorated with a frill and dried flowers half way down. The church was really colourful, from the iconostasis that shone in the candlelight to the rich velvety robes of the Papas, and the silver covered bible.

No hymns were sung during the service, but we listened to soothing chanting from the priest and choir. We wore linked crowns; ours were twisted circles of white porcelain roses linked by a ribbon. The Koubaros (best man) swapped the crowns on our heads during the service - nervously he did it about ten times until the papas finally stopped him. The priest led us in the 'Dance of Isaiah', three times around the altar table, with the best man continuing to hold the crowns above our heads. Meanwhile the congregation threw rice at us (a symbol of fertility), as the priest kept his bible strategically in front of him to avoid being hit in the face! Even though there were not many at our wedding, we were showered in rice from three large bags - our hair was full of it and later I even found grains in my underwear.

As the service was brought to a close we shook hands with our guests and handed out *koufeta*, prettily decorated silk bags with sugared almonds, customarily given at Greek baptisms and weddings. As we went out onto the church steps our UK guests threw traditional British confetti and rose petals.

We spent part of our honeymoon in **Perdika** (Πέρδικα), a quiet fishing village 9 km south of the main town. The wife of the hotel owner, knowing we had just got married, decorated our bed with a beautiful lace bedspread scattered with rice and rose petals. A couple of wedding guests, involved with this surprise, placed money on the bed - another Greek custom.

Perdika was a great place to stay. We had lovely views of the **Islet of Moni** (N. Μονή) directly opposite the village. In the summer months boats make the 10 minute trip regularly to the uninhabited islet, where there is a seasonal taverna, a good beach and lots of wildlife.

Another attraction of Perdika has to be its *psaro tavernas*. It is famous for these seafood restaurants where the fish is served almost from the net to the plate. Nothing is frozen, even the kalamari that on most menus have an asterisk to indicate *katapsimenos* (frozen) is straight from the sea. Our reception was at one of these restaurants. We feasted on a bouillabaisse fish soup, cuttle fish (soupiés) in a tomato sauce, squid, octopus, a selection of grilled meats for the meat lovers, plus salads and plenty of local wine flowing. The festivities continued at our hotel in the evening, with champagne and the cutting of a traditional British wedding cake.

Since our wedding we have visited Perdika several times, although on short trips we find it more convenient to stay in the main town, or **Faros** (Φάρος) a 15 minute walk away on the outskirts.

We have also stayed in **Aghia Marina**, considered the island's main resort because it has the best beach. Long and sandy, it's ideal for young children as the sea does not get deep quickly, so they can paddle a long way out. To us, with just one main street lined with bars and souvenir shops, it lacks character and is not as appealing as Aegina Town or Perdika. However, it does have one big advantage, being close to the impressive Doric **Temple of Aphaia** (Ναός Αφαίας). This is my favourite ancient site and a 'must' to see.

Aphaia is older than the Parthenon and you can enjoy it without the crowds that amass at the Acropolis. We have often had the site to ourselves to sit in peace admiring the temple and the surrounding pine clad hills. From the hill top there are fantastic views of the Aegean and on a clear day it is possible to see both the Acropolis and Sounion. The very positioning of these ancient sites is the subject of much debate as the three Doric temples were built in the same period, from 480 to 444BC, forming an isosceles triangle on a map. Was this intentional?

Usually after wandering around the site we sit at the pleasant café opposite, at the stone tables and benches in the shade if it is hot. It is also good to rest here if you have walked from Aghia Marina.

If you visit the temple from the main town, at the village of **Kondos** (Κοντός) you will pass the **Monastery of Aghios Nektarious**, Aegina's patron saint. It is a place of pilgrimage, particularly on 9th November, the special day dedicated to Saint Nektarios. You cannot miss the church for two reasons - it is one of the biggest churches in the Balkans, but also, if you are travelling by bus, you will notice that lots of ladies dressed in black, wearing gold crucifixes, get off at this stop. At last you will have a chance to take a seat instead of hanging on for dear life as the bus speeds along the winding roads that cut

through pine covered hills and fields of pistachio and almond trees.

Palea Hora (Παλαιά Χώρα), the 'old town', is also worth a visit. Near to Agios Nektarios, the islanders lived here amongst the hills from the 9th to 19th c. AD for protection from pirate raids. It is Aegina's equivalent to Mystras in the Peloponnese, and is like a ghost town - maybe with some lingering ghosts! Wandering along the trails amongst the ancient buildings and crumbling churches it can feel quite eerie. We have been inside some of the small churches, which are open but often quite neglected, although the frescoes and icons are very impressive. Sadly graffiti of pirate boats and skull-and-crossbones spoils some of the icons and the eyes of some Saints have been scratched out. Who knows whether this is ancient or modern day graffiti, but it is a sad desecration.

Back in Aegina town we often enjoy a leisurely *volta* along the seafront past the colourful caiques. These are not only fishing boats, some are used as greengrocery shops displaying fruit and vegetables. It makes such a lovely picture that it features on some postcards in the tourist shops. As we pass these boats we are encouraged to sample the island's fresh pistachio nuts. We invariably end up buying a few bags to take home, or sample a few as we continue past the marina, which is normally full of yachts. On our last visit we sat on the wall to watch a fisherman tenderising an octopus he had caught by banging it repeatedly and energetically against the rocks.

We eventually head over to our favourite ouzeri, one street in from the seafront, adjacent to the fish market. We grab a table, next to the barbecue if we can, to watch Yiannis grilling octopus and stuffed kalamari over the hot coals. It always amuses us to watch him. His main piece of equipment is a battered and grimy hairdryer which he uses to rekindle the coals. Often we sit there for hours listening to the local fishermen discussing what they caught that day or their opinions on local politics. If we are lucky, as it gets late and the ouzo has flowed sufficiently, someone will bring out a bouzouki and play island songs. We relax and drink barrelled wine and enjoy the moreish fish mezethes they serve. The only thing we have to think about is whether to visit Aghia Marina tomorrow, or perhaps take a water taxi to the neighbouring island of Agistri just 25 minutes away, or just stay in Aegina Town soaking up the atmosphere of this, our special island.

How to get to Aegina

By Air - Scheduled or charter flights to Athens, then ferry / hydrofoil

By Ferry/Hydrofoil - Piraeus, Agistri
- occasional excursions to Epidavros, Hydra, Methana & Poros.

Package Tour Operators - Hidden Greece, Island Wandering, Rediscover Greece, Seafarer, Sunisle.

Holidaying with Friends *by Kay Holston*

Our first trip to Greece was with two very close friends, to the isle of **Skiathos** during the last week of the season. The year was ... oh, I can't remember ... but it began a flirtation with this wonderful country, lifestyle and people, that is now a love affair.

First, however, I have to confess that on arrival I found the accommodation very sparse and the toilet situation, to a newcomer like myself, very odd. I did wonder how we were going to survive it. But realistically, what was the concern? We had all that anyone could need on a sunshine holiday plus the camaraderie of friends to add to our enjoyment.

The first memorable trip with our friends, took us by bus to the fabulous **Koukounaries** beach, miles long and served by ample tavernas, just paces away from the loungers. Mel (now my husband) and Bill had learned of a lake behind the beach and prepared to investigate the wildlife. They made their way back to us, disappointed, as it wasn't the fresh water inlet they had thought. As they returned to where Lynn and I were warming through to medium rare, two buxom (and topless) young ladies giggled as they showered away the sand and watched our intrepid explorers approach wearing floppy hats, sandals, long shorts, baggy T-shirts, huge binoculars around their necks and trying hard not to look at the ladies' assets. Lynn and I wondered if they might walk straight past us, but alas, we had to admit ownership.

The best event was on the penultimate day of our stay. It had rained all morning as though Noah was in residence, so we decided to siesta until the sun broke through to chase the wet patches from the patio. Mel and I gathered our things and headed for the pool. After the rain, it was pretty chilled but we endured it (despite goose bumps) as we waited for Bill and Lynn to join us. Neither before, nor since, have we ever seen anyone bungee jump in and out of a pool so fast, without the aid of elastic!

Our next vacation with the long suffering Bill and Lynn took us to **Zakynthos**. Arriving at the apartments about noon, whilst unpacking, we were oblivious to the ominous cloud creeping through the clear blue sky. Unperturbed, we all made our way to the bar, taking fleece jackets, as the air felt a little nippy. Then it happened - the heavens let down their wrath ... but we remained, resilient, huddled under a parasol whilst rivulets of rain crashed like moving stalactites to the floor. The pool looked as though it was coming to the boil as the raindrops bubbled up on landing in the water. An hour later the storm had passed and the temperature rose. With the quickening sunshine, the tempest was soon forgotten.

Storms seemed to be the order of the day with us on this island. Come

Wednesday night, the clouds sought us out again and gave us the most spectacular light show, often without the stair rods of rain. We witnessed at least three storms, all doing battle as the twilight made a backdrop for the ensuing war that crashed and stamped across the sky.

One afternoon, our lads (both on the wrong side of forty, of portly build but still capable of wearing out a Scalextric) decided to make the most of the airbeds and the empty pool. Commandeering two air beds they tried to straddle them from the poolside; then lined two up, end to end, to run across; then attempting to surf Hawaii 5-O style across the pool providing endless entertainment for all - two fat guys playing with the kids' toys. The finale saw Mel jumping onto one whilst Bill held it steady - but he pulled it away at the very last second. Mel, usually so prepared, was not this time!

Relaxing in Naxos - Robert with Kay & Mel

June 2005, we travelled to **Naxos** with my brother, Robert and wife, Bronwen, meeting up with friends Sue and Steve, who were already there. Sue had already booked for us both to go horse riding for three hours. I was not looking forward to spending such a long time in the saddle.

First morning, we awoke to the clatter of pans, enthused laughter and the smell of bacon wafting on the air from next door. Mel, languishing in contentment, piped up *"Quiet holiday? Sounds like we've brought the cast of Carry On Camping with us !"* It will be no surprise that they are now fondly and regularly known as Sid and Hattie.

We took S & H for a Greek dancing night at a harbour restaurant, The Flamingo, one night. As we entered, I practised my pidgin Greek *"Ena trapezie yia tessera, parakalo."* The reply came in a broad cockney accent *"Alright love, this way,"* to booming laughter from S & H. As Mel was catching us up a little later, it gave me the chance to suggest that Mel can do a fire dance. Sue and Steve joined us after their meal too, and a free carafe of wine was provided to stall us - couldn't think why?

Then the hosts of the restaurant grabbed me (this wasn't part of the plan) and I was invited to join in a very demure ladies dance which involves following the leader (as far as I know) but the locals seemed pleased that I participated and then ...

Mel was the star of the show! Holding up his arms in the form of a dying sea gull, they squirted lighter fluid around and set it alight so there was no escape. A waiter sat on Mel's back after getting him to do press-ups and he collapsed to the floor to peals of appreciative laughter. After a few seconds he was lifted to his feet by the back of his collar to finish with a finale of leaping (sort of) into the air and slapping both feet at the same time to a much deserved roar of applause and hoots from an audience of visitors and locals alike. We have it on video for disbelievers.

The pool at these apartments was also entertaining, especially as the poolside bar was quite derelict. It had a vine branch about 5 inches thick, growing through the middle of it, rendering the fridge door impossible to open. We brought our own bar in cool bags, so cheap beer and wine were plentiful. This was also where Bronwen made her mark - lying unsuspiciously on a lounger, complete with shorts, T-shirt, baseball cap and sunglasses to lull us into a sense of security, she would suddenly launch herself, lifeboat style, into the water to attack her basking prey, leaving onlookers flailing around with laughter whilst, on this occasion, Mel floundered in the pool.

Then, there was the marathon horse ride that Sue had booked. We were collected near to the apartments and duly given our steeds, mine a narrow, chestnut thoroughbred and Sue's a grey Connemara type. We walked on paths through a bamboo 'jungle' (as our German escorts referred to it) protecting the fields from the Meltemi wind.

"Now we shall twot," announced our escort. I looked at Sue, who, like me, was stifling a grunting giggle. The bamboo seemed to go on forever but

eventually we got to a beach, bathed the horses' hooves in the cool water and stopped at a taverna. Propping ourselves at the bar, we ordered drinks - luckily I only ordered a half (with my brothers I have learned from the men and not the boys!). Halfway through we heard a shout *"We go now!"* I guzzled my beer down thinking I needed a toilet stop before trying to haul myself back up on this poor creature. A German girl held the offside stirrup whilst I swung Tarzan-like on the near side stirrup trying to swing my arthritic hip and

knee across the horse. After a half jump, half push from another German girl, I was mounted. An hour later it was all over and I had survived - just waiting for the aches to set in. Sure enough, the following morning my legs felt as though I'd tried to crack coconuts with them.

Sue and Steve left early on the Saturday morning along with the people they befriended in their first week. It did seem quiet; Rob was unusually subdued and Bronwen wasn't in the mood for her Jaws routine, but Rob's birthday would be soon, so we started to make plans for the celebration. We chose a courtyard restaurant near to the old town, sunken from the street and with an intimate but convivial ambience.

That night the carafes of wine and beers kept coming. Rob was getting warmed up again and Bron had the video camera. With 'Our Sid' centre stage, we didn't know what he would come out with, but we could bet on it being something to make us cringe - oh well.

It can be more fun holidaying with friends, but, I would recommend the following points for discussion *before* you go away:

1. *Agree to allow each other privacy and room for individual movement.*

2. *Don't take offence if your friends want to do something different. It's their holiday.*

3. *Don't feel rail-roaded into doing things you don't want to do. It's your holiday too.*

4. *As much as you may love your companions, you cannot possibly agree 100% of the time, so agree to disagree and move on.*

5. *This rule probably belongs to another article, but may apply to folk who purchase a holiday home - although I'm sure you want to share your home, make ground rules about what you would like your guests to help with, especially as we all have different 'little ways' (mine is laundry). However, please remember, however hard, it is still their holiday.*

6. *Just get out there and enjoy every moment, because afterwards is too late, and friendships are much too precious.*

We've had some great times on holidays with friends, but all relationships need care and consideration. The people we have mentioned have a similar mind set to us. Our family are also friends and we are lucky enough to have friends we consider as family. We have their blessing on this article and we would like to say *"Efharisto para poli"* for giving and sharing many fantastic times with us. Mel and I hope there will be many more - especially when we make 'Ag. Nectarios' on Kos our only home.

Aegean Balcony *by Fiona Collingwood*

Tranquillity ...
There is a stillness that seems to enclose me like a vacuum.
My senses glory in what I can see from my small balcony.
The sun has only recently risen over the island
and bathes everything in golden light,
opening flowers, making simple whitewashed houses grand abodes.
It washes my skin and relaxes my body and mind.

Geranium and bougainvillea spill from terracotta pots,
trying to make a pathway to the sea, which laps softly underneath.
Brightly coloured fishing boats are now returning to the harbour
and gulls dive into the hues of green and blue,
the sea matching the church domes
which glint proudly in the morning sun.

I watch the papas, clothed from head to toe in black,
hobbling along the narrow cobbled lanes,
grasping a large metal key ready to open the church for morning service.
Soon I will hear the church bells peeling.
Just behind the priest is old Maria,
leading a donkey to the harbour at the bottom of the volcanic cliffs,
ready to take the many tourists who come to this beautiful isle,
up the steep slopes.

The island is waking.
The smell of freshly baked bread, koulourakia and tiropites
wafts from the nearby fournos, mingling with
the ever present scent of basil and thyme.
I rise slowly from my chair and with much reluctance
leave my Aegean balcony.

'Nothing' to Drink *by Fr. Anastasios D. Salapatas*

On the anniversary of the Greek Independence Day on 25th.March 2004, at the end of a very interesting function of the Peloponnesian Association of Great Britain held at the Hellenic Centre in Central London, in the midst of a quite joyful audience, the Chairman of the Association (Fr. A.D. Salapatas) thanking the speaker, Mr. Costas Cavvadas, for his excellent presentation, said among other words the following:

"…You have offered us everything tonight, we would like to offer you a 'nothing' ".

Everybody was absolutely silent in the Great Hall. The chairman looking around at the surprised faces, continued his thanksgiving speech by saying *"I didn't say that we would like to offer you 'nothing', but a 'nothing' ".* Then he took in his hands a box and offered it to the stunned speaker and explained to the audience what he meant.

The box contained a bottle of drink, which is called 'Nothing'. In Greek 'Tipota' (Τίποτα). It is a drink produced in the heart of Peloponnese, in Tripolis, since 1949.

A clever Peloponnesian man, the distiller Nicholas Biris, had started making it as a response to those who would answer *"nothing thanks"* when asked whether they would like something to drink.

"From now on anyone who says 'nothing thanks' when I offer him a drink gets a shot of my brandy, even if I have to pour it down his throat. 'You asked for it, I'll tell him'", Biris said.

The Daily Oklahoman in March 1957 dedicated an article to this drink which reads:

"So what does TIPOTA taste like? It tastes like the best brandy I have ever had. (Not too difficult since I can't stand brandy). It tastes like almonds and vanilla and is kind of sweet. Well actually it is really sweet but it is really good too. TIPOTA is sold in Tripolis and probably around Athens if you ask in liquor stores but we found our bottle at a fast-food travel stop on the National Road on the way to Tripolis. Drink it cold".

It is still produced in Tripolis in different bottle sizes. I am not certain of its price at the moment nor where to buy it outside this area.

Greek Food for Health *by Sylvia Cook*

We have all heard that the Mediterranean diet contains all the elements needed for good health - high in the use of vegetables, pulses, fish, yoghourt, olive oil, and traditionally with meat in much lower quantities than is generally the case today in the western diet. Many of the foods grown in Greece are also purported to have specific health giving properties and are recommended as remedies for specific complaints or to maintain good health.

In ancient times Greek doctors knew the power of natural produce. Hippocrates (470 - 330 BC), the 'Father of Modern Medicine', was the first to classify about 600 useful plants as medicinal remedies. Many are still used to good effect today. It is commendable that we are turning again to the fruits of the land, which have fewer harmful side effects than many chemically produced remedies. I'm not a nutritionist nor a doctor, just someone who believes that some natural remedies and a healthy diet can work. These are just some of the claims made by many for foods and herbs commonly found in Greece.

sc

Basil - From the Greek word for king, as well as imparting a unique flavour particularly in tomato dishes, this herb has sedative properties and an infusion will help clear stomach cramps and sickness. Basil helps reduce stress, is a good digestive and appetite stimulant, as well as easing constipation. I have also read that it is an aphrodisiac. I can never resist pinching a leaf or two when passing a pot of basil to rub between my fingers and inhale the refreshing aroma and I love to add torn basil leaves to fresh sun-ripened Greek tomatoes, drizzled with good olive oil and a dash of balsamic vinegar.

Chamomile - Usually taken as an infusion or herbal tea, but also as oil extracted from the flowers, chamomile has calming and soothing properties particularly for stomach cramps and painful menstruation. The infusion can also be used externally as an antiseptic, anti-inflammatory and anti-allergy wash or poultice - particularly good for sensitive or intimate parts of the body to relieve itchy conditions. Thriving in Greece on waste ground, chamomile is another Greek named plant - from 'apple of the ground' for its fragrant apple scent. It is also said to aid the recovery of unhealthy plants grown alongside it.

Cinnamon - Mostly grown in Asia, but used extensively in east Mediterranean sweet and savoury cooking for its warm spicy flavour, the bark of the cinnamon tree is a also a circulation stimulant and an astringent for clearing nose and lungs, often used combined with ginger in cooking and remedies. Simply chew a stick of cinnamon to bring relief from nose

colds, or drink warm milk with honey and a teaspoon or two of ground cinnamon at bedtime.

Cucumber - To cool the body as a food or applied externally, cucumber is also a diuretic. Sore eyes can be relieved simply by resting with a slice of cucumber over each closed eye, or rub the juice directly into the skin to cool the effect of sunburn or a fever. It is used extensively in skin lotions too.

Dill - Called 'anithos' in Greek, dill has stomach soothing properties, aids digestion and is often used in children's medicines (eg. gripe water). The seeds have a pungent flavour and can be chewed to cure bad breath. The feathery leaves (also called dill-weed) are chopped and added to sauces, vegetables or fish, or in pickles. Try mixing with butter to serve on hot baked potatoes.

Garlic & Onions - Including good quantities of both these edible bulbs in your diet will thin the blood (making it less prone to clotting), lower cholesterol and blood sugar levels and help clear chest infections and blocked noses. Onion or garlic juice are strong antiseptics for external use on spots, wounds and for fungal and ear infections. An onion poultice can help draw splinters, or clean wounds - roast a whole onion until soft, cut in half and apply to the affected area. Crushed garlic with lemon juice can cure warts and verrucas.

Figs - Nourishing and easily digested, figs are probably best known medicinally for their laxative qualities, often prescribed as syrup of figs, but a few dried figs chopped and added to breakfast muesli or cereals will provide a gentle laxative to avoid constipation if taken regularly. Used since ancient times, mashed or roasted and cut in half, they make a poultice for boils and skin diseases.

Honey - The predigested sugars in honey make it easily available to nourish a body weakened by flu or other ailments. It also takes on some of the properties of the plants from which it was gathered, eg. thyme. Externally its antiseptic and drawing properties can soothe raw or itching rashes on skin and clean wounds.

Lemons - The skin, zest, oil and juice of lemons provide invaluable remedies - for colds (with honey), to cleanse the liver, to cool the digestive system and aid elimination of toxins, and externally as an antiseptic on bites and astringent healing lotion for chapped skin when combined with honey and oil. Drink a little lemon juice in water if prone to nose bleeds, or as a healthy appetite suppressant when dieting.

Olive Oil - Pressed from ripe olives, olive oil's mono-unsaturated fat lowers harmful LDL cholesterol, yet leaves beneficial HDL cholesterol alone. It contains anti oxidants and vitamin E, lowers the risk of heart disease and stimulates the production of bile, helping to maintain the gall bladder and liver.

Oregano - This Greek herb tastes good in any hot dish with a tomato sauce and is an aid to digestion. As an infusion it is good to relieve the symptoms of colds and flu.

Parsley - Flat or curly leaved parsley aids digestion, hence its use as a garnish or chopped in sauces. It is also helpful in reducing water retention (diuretic), inflamed kidneys and regulating periods. In WWI it was given to soldiers in the trenches as a tea to combat the after effects on the kidneys of dysentery. It relieves stress, headaches and cramps and is a useful antidote to the unpleasant effect of garlic on the breath. A symbol of strength to ancient Greeks, winners' garlands at athletic games were often made of parsley.

Pistachio Nuts - Brought to Greece from the Middle East, Pistachio nuts are high in protein and mono-unsaturated fats, B & E vitamins and minerals - particularly potassium. They can help protect against high blood pressure and cholesterol and have an anti inflammatory effect.

Pomegranates - With its abundance of seeds, this unique fruit was a symbol for 'wedded love and fruitfulness' in ancient times. More recent confirmation that it contains bioflavonoids and other antioxidants, makes it useful in guarding against chronic degenerative diseases.

SC

Purslane - Often found growing wild in Greece, purslane contains omega 3 fatty acids which strengthen the immune system. The leaves also contain vitamin C, calcium, carotene, iron, thiamin, riboflavin and niacin and taste great fresh, sprinkled over a 'horiatiki' in season.

Rosemary - Inhale rosemary oil if you are feeling faint, or massage with infused oil to treat dandruff, itchy scalp or aching muscles. Drink rosemary tea with lemon juice daily to improve circulation and varicose veins - said to strengthen the memory too as it improves blood flow to the head and stimulates the nervous system. It also makes a good breath freshener as a mouthwash.

Sage - Antiseptic, antiviral and antibacterial, sage also has decongestant properties. Sage is recognised as a natural ingredient to ease the hot flushes of the menopause, or with peppermint as a tea to help clear blocked sinuses. Use a strong sage tea as a mouthwash or gargle to alleviate mouth disorders, adding honey and lemon for a sore throat. A sage and vinegar poultice can ease strains - the vinegar brings bruising to the surface whilst sage assists with soothing and reducing swelling.

Salt - We all know we should minimise our salt intake to reduce high blood pressure, but salt is an essential element of our diet, especially when exposed to high temperatures and loss of salt through sweating. Its main power medicinally is external - as a gentle antiseptic diluted in water to cleanse even the most delicate areas, or as a mouthwash. A dip in the sea (or a sea-salt bath) will cleanse wounds, relieve tiredness or stiffness and clear impurities excreted through the skin. Follow with a rinse in clear cool water.

Thyme - Strongly antiseptic and antibacterial, thyme helps clear sinuses (expectorant) and calms nerves and depression. A sprig of thyme or splash of thyme oil in bath water can relieve fatigue, or use in cooking with rich foods as a digestive with a wonderful aroma, also said to delay the onset of age related deterioration of muscles, brain function and the retina. A thyme infused oil massaged on the chest or thyme tea taken internally can relieve a chesty cough. For a household disinfectant with a unique thyme smell, fill a large jar with thyme, cover with wine vinegar, leave in the sun 40 days, strain vinegar, discard thyme and replace with fresh thyme for another 40 days.

Walnuts - Walnuts are rich in antioxidants and omega 3 fatty acids, Vitamin E and minerals - good for tissue growth, to combat stress and high LDL cholesterol. Pickle walnuts when green and soft (the poisonous cyanide they contain at this stage is destroyed by pickling). Gargling with the vinegar will soothe sore throats and the young pickled walnuts are a good source of Vitamin C too.

Yoghourt - 'Friendly' probiotic bacteria in yoghourt enhance your immune system - in particular for intestinal health, aiding the fight against harmful bacteria that can cause diarrhoea, reducing risk of colon cancer and lowering blood cholesterol levels. It's also soothing spread on sunburn - and Greek yoghourt undoubtedly tastes the best!

Cooking for Theo by Tony Brown

If there is one character who had a profound influence, not only on my career in catering but also on my whole attitude to 'grecofilia', it is restaurateur, entrepreneur and philosopher, Theophilus Alaveras of Crete.

I'd been running out of money and hanging round his Neo Restaurant Bar for what seemed like an age, and although I hadn't actually lied, I'd puffed up my experience and knowledge of the culinary arts enough to make myself seem like an irreplaceable asset in a town full of restaurants. Then before his trip to Kassos, Theo decided to take me on.

He showed me round the kitchen, told me to forget everything I'd ever been taught before, then proceeded to re-educate me in the art of cooking for crowds. He put a hand on each shoulder, looked me in the eyes, his waxed moustache dangerously pointing east and west, and announced with his customary doleful expression, *"Listen to me, Antonis. You might not make much money here, but then I don't charge for training."*

He not only sharpened my humour, he also gave me myself.

Theophilus

At five the next evening I turned up for work and stood in front of the stove, closed my eyes, held my breath and leapt into the abyss of catering à la carte, promising to emulate Theo's own seemingly effortless style for at least the next fourteen nights and hopefully longer.

During those two weeks, I abandoned my own path and followed the Theo way of cooking under pressure. No drinking, late nights or being late. He encouraged lots of fresh air and moderation in everything. *"You will become a thinker in my kitchen. Either the customer wins or you do - you decide!"*

He encouraged trust in my sense of smell and helped me develop a discriminating array of taste buds. He instilled the necessity of blending colour and texture, and as far as the blade and the block were concerned, I gained finesse with a razor's edge.

"You have only eight fingers and two thumbs. Don't waste any of them." Every day there were words of wisdom. *"Never use a clock. Let your sixth sense alert you when cooking time is over."* It was impossible not to feel younger than him - he was as wise as the ancient hills around us.

Looking back, it was either a calculated risk or his own reckless sense of humour that caused him, the owner of one of the most prestigious restaurants in southern Crete, to take me on trial as his cover chef but secretly, I

suspect Theo simply enjoyed teaching life's lessons and taking risks. He rarely lost his temper, but step out of line and you sensed his disappointment. Calmly, he would take control, appeal to your intellect and leave you to work out where you went wrong.

For instance, on one occasion he became so suspicious of his bar manager diverting the takings that he simply promoted him to cash controller and made him responsible for every drachma. Miraculously, the money stopped disappearing, the manager took the credit and the staff were relieved.

Theo's humour was sharp. You never knew when he was pulling your leg.

He was known to swan through the kitchen on the way to the bar showering advice on his assistants right and left. *"Attention everybody! Listen to me! Never slice anything so thick you can't see through it"* or, giggling and clapping his hands like a flamenco dancer, *"Come now, clear 'Table 2' - we're running out of lettuce! Come on!"*

I believe he placed great faith in his instincts. *"If the boss is content, the establishment runs itself."*

He let us drink as much as we dared. The penalty for being 'tired and emotional' was instant dismissal, but since everybody loved Theophilus, no one let him down.

There were times when he came close to disaster. One of his kitchen rules was that any home-made soup left over from the day before was placed in the bottom of the fridge to be thrown away by the kitchen assistant - he never took chances with food.

One evening at the height of his performance, he was told a rather pompous gentleman diner wanted to see him with regard to the soup. *"But there is no soup on tonight's menu."* He raised his eyes to the gods. Then, believing attack is the strongest form of defence, presented himself at table with a huge smile, *"Good evening sir, everything to your liking, yes?"*

"Well, this soup has an alcoholic bite and I was wondering if it might be past its best." The man's hungry family, each with a bowl of the suspect soup before them, stared with admiration at their father then turned and waited on the next words from Theo. He fell silent, then smiled warmly.

"Many of my customers make that mistake. You see, we use an old Cretan recipe and just before we serve the soup, I throw in a glass of traditional Cretan raki for good luck. This may have confused you."

"Oh, well that`s fine. It really is most unusual. Thank you."

Theophilus sailed back into the kitchen and took a sword down from the wall. *"Bring me the kitchen assistant. Immediately!"*

We were a good team and took great pride in accepting responsibility and running the restaurant ourselves whenever Theo and his wife, Tsaly were away. It was theatre, and the show must go on. We worked hard and late, had some fun and usually all went well.

... But pride often comes before a fall. At the end of those two weeks my rump hit the ground with a mighty thump. It was on Theo's return from Kassos that he came to me, shook my hand and simply said, *"Antonis, I'm impressed. Have a night off."* A night off? Unheard of in summer.

That evening I rewarded myself with a Psarosoupa, a favourite soup in Crete (see recipes) and a bottle of fine white Cretan wine at a table for one on my balcony, overlooking the summer evening street. For the first time in over a fortnight I let out a long sigh and relaxed. I was just wallowing in my own conceit when a loud banging on my door shattered the peace and quiet.

There stood a furious Theophilus, feet apart, hands flaying the air, eyes wide with anger. *"Mister Brown, as you know, we sell lamb, chicken, veal, biftekia, brisoles, lamb chops, souvlakia, moussaka and we open in just half an hour. Now since you forgot to take any of these from the freezer for tonight's menu dear boy, that means we've got no goddam meat. Nothing!"*

Economy with words, yet his condemnation hung like the sword of Damocles as he wheeled round and stormed off, leaving me to make a panic-stricken circuit of the other restaurants in the hope of finding replacements. Time was running out but I was in luck and managed to gather not just an ample selection of unfrozen vital main course ingredients, but also some very flattering praise from Cleo's Restaurant, our biggest rival in the town.

By the time I returned to our kitchen I was bursting at the seams with pride and self-esteem, declaring to all and sundry as I pushed open the door, *"The 7th Cavalry's arrived!"*

Silence. You could cut the air with a carving knife. *"And guess what Theo? Cleo herself offered me a job!"*

He deflated my triumph in an instant. *"What as? Stock Controller?"*

The incident was never mentioned again and The Neo became my home from home for the rest of the summer. When the time came to say my goodbyes and catch the bus to Iraklio, Theo and I stood on the veranda overlooking the rooftops in a moment of silent reflection. Then he turned to me and said softly, *"Antonis, why must you go back to England? I don't understand. Here you have a good job, the Cretan sky, the Libyan sea and*

a wonderful lifestyle - but most of all, you have my friendship. So why?"

I couldn't answer. We hugged and as I lumbered down the steps towards the square, my tears fell in buckets.

Since then, I have dropped in several times with my wife and always enjoyed the special treatment Theo reserves for his guests of honour and like the old guru master that he is, he always leaves it for me to mention my big disgrace before we laugh and cry, and laugh about it all over again.

To conjure up memories of the *worst* week of my life (at the Neo while Theo was in Kassos), is not such a pleasant experience for me - but if the story is to be told at all it must be told in full.

For all his largesse, pseudo-palikaria and filleting wit, if there was one person in the Alaveras household who could stop Theo in his tracks and reduce him to an ingratiating, fawning, grovelling flunky, it was Stavroula, his mother. A burly lady in her mid-sixties with grey streaked hair dragged into a bun, soft complexion with emerging goatee and a look that could cut through steel, she would appear without warning and simply stand in the doorway with her right index finger raised, smile generously and say, 'Ena'. This was meant to indicate she was about to begin her inspection, and if she found anything she didn't like she wouldn't hesitate in letting it be known - although sometimes, if she was in a particularly bad mood, she would say nothing and simply stand in the doorway until the last poor wretch in the kitchen cottoned on, then she would sweep through the rooms like a cyclone and be gone without a word. Some time later, there would be a talk from Theo and changes would be announced.

I had met her only briefly in the week before I started and I don't think I gave her a thought. Then Theo departed and I was in the kitchen alone, well, except for Kosmas the waiter and a young couple from Belgium, who were the kitchen helps and waiters. Stavroula appeared and decided she would show me how *she* expected the kitchen to run. I was to forget everything Theophilus had told me, she would train me in *her* way.

I won't go into detail about the look in her eyes when I asked her to remove little Stavrouli and her friend from the kitchen whilst I was chopping sides of lamb with an axe, or the time she threw a pan of fried chips across the kitchen at me and told me that from that moment I was only to do the washing up, or my gloom, or how I cried myself to sleep *(only joking)*, but to say I was pleased when Theophilus returned would be like saying Perseus was pleased when he decapitated Medusa.

I don't think I saw her again after he came home and maybe in recompense, Theo took me on for the season.

However, if there is one thing I learned from Stavroula it is that most traditional Cretan cooking contains little meat and since I prefer fish, vegetables and fruit too, I would like to include a couple of her favourite recipes here for you to try.

Psarosoupa Medusa - Medusa's Fish Soup by *Tony Brown*

Follow the recipe and invite your friends round... (enough for 5-6 people)

> *1 - 1.5 kg / 2½ - 3 lbs mixed Sea Creatures (any size fish, octopus, sardines, smelts, etc)*
>
> *2.5 litres / 4 pints Water*
>
> *2 large Onions, sliced*
>
> *2 Carrots, diced*
>
> *2 stalks Celery, chopped*
>
> *large bunch of Parsley, chopped*
>
> *Salt & Pepper*
>
> *½ cup Olive Oil*
>
> *4 Potatoes, diced*

Method:

- ❏ Just clean and wash the fish. Cut big ones into thick slices, leave small ones whole, cut octopus if used into serving size pieces.
- ❏ Boil water in a large saucepan. Add the onions, carrots, celery, most of the parsley, salt, pepper and oil. Return to boil & simmer for 45 mins.
- ❏ Add the pieces of fish and the potatoes. Simmer for another 15 mins.

Serve, sprinkled with fresh parsley, accompanied with fresh crusty bread.

Nerantzi Glyko - Bitter Orange Peel Preserve *by Tony Brown*

I love these when I need a sugar-boost. The orange pith loses its bitterness with the soaking and boiling and the discarded orange pulp tastes great mixed with Greek yoghourt. (It does work with ordinary oranges if you can't get hold of bitter oranges.)

10 thick-skinned Bitter Oranges - Peel and Pith only

1.4 kilos / 3 lbs Sugar

600 ml / 1 pint Water

Juice of 1 Lemon

140ml / ¼ pint Glucose Syrup

Method

❏ Grate orange skins lightly to remove zest. Rinse and cut the oranges top to bottom into sixths. Discard the orange pulp.

❏ Roll up each sixth piece tightly and using a needle, thread 15 rolls together and tie at the ends of the thread to prevent unrolling.

❏ Put the rings of peel in a large saucepan with plenty of cold water and leave soaking until the following day.

❏ Drain and pour fresh water over. Boil the rolls until tender, changing the water at least twice to remove bitterness. (I usually boil for an hour, change water, then another hour before testing on my teeth - but it will vary with oranges and to personal taste). Drain and remove the threads.

❏ Boil the 600 ml (1 pint) of water with the sugar for a few minutes, then add the orange peel rolls. Boil for 15 minutes, remove from the heat and leave in the syrup until next day.

❏ Take out peel rolls with fork or slotted spoon and set aside. Boil syrup again until it is thick and slides off the spoon in sheets - like lightning. Add the lemon juice, glucose syrup, then the orange peel rolls.

❏ Simmer for a few minutes more until thick again and 'sheets' off the spoon as before.

❏ Store in glass jars and serve cold as a 'spoon' sweet.

Adapted from Tony Brown's website www.grecofilia.co.uk

Beetroot Salad/Pantzaria Salata *by Sylvia Cook*

One of the best parts of beetroot 'salad' (as the Greeks call many vegetable dishes served cold or warm) παντζάρια in Greek, is the part we usually throw away in Britain. The stems and leaves are served alongside the beetroot bulbs and taste like a sweeter version of spinach. Perhaps because they grow more quickly in the warmth of a Greek winter and spring, the leaves are more tender than they may be back home, or perhaps they are just available more fresh as the leaves can wither quickly after pulling from the ground.

You can leave out a few of the larger bulbs to slice and pickle in a little wine vinegar if you also enjoy beetroot this way.

Large bunch of fresh beetroot complete with leaves

Salt

Lemon juice

Olive oil

Method

- ☐ Put large saucepan of salted water to boil.

- ☐ Cut beetroot bulbs off stems just above base leaving root on (to minimise 'bleeding'). Scrub clean and place in boiling water until tender - 30-40 mins depending on size.

- ☐ Meanwhile cut stalks and leaves across bunch into 2-3 pieces and wash.

- ☐ Take cooked bulbs out of water and rinse under cold tap. Slip off and discard skins, tops and roots.

- ☐ Meanwhile, immerse stems in the boiling water, simmer 5 minutes. Add leaves and simmer a further 5 minutes.

- ☐ Strain and serve on a platter with small beets cut in quarters, large ones sliced. Sprinkle liberally with lemon juice and a good olive oil.

Often served with 'skordalia', a garlic and potato sauce.

Pastitsio *by Gill Tomlinson*

(From Greek Taverna Cookbook - chef's recipes from Kefalonia see reviews p166)

This recipe, courtesy of Spiros from Katelios Taverna, produces a very fine *pastitsio*. Allow to stand to firm up for a few moments after removing from the oven. If you do have any leftovers, by the time it is completely cooled it will slice into lovely big taverna-style slabs. (Serves 4, takes 2 hours)

> *250g/ 9oz Pastitsio Pasta No 2 or 3*
> *50g/ 2oz Kefalotiri Cheese, grated*

For Meat Sauce:
> *1 Onion, finely chopped*
> *2 cloves Garlic, crushed*
> *2 tablesp Olive Oil*
> *375g / 13oz Minced Beef*
> *250g / 8oz Tomatoes*
> *Tomato Puree*
> *1 Bay Leaf*
> *Handful fresh Parsley, chopped*
> *Salt & Pepper*

For Bechamel Sauce:
> *500ml / 17.5 fl. oz Milk*
> *40g/ 1.5oz Butter*
> *40g / 1.5oz Flour*
> *50g/2oz Kefalotiri Cheese,grated*
> *2 pinches Nutmeg*
> *Salt & White Pepper*
> *1 Egg*

Method

- ❑ Fry onion and garlic in olive oil until soft. Add mince and cook for a few minutes to brown it.

- ❑ Chop the tomatoes in a food processor and pour onto the mince. Add a little tomato puree if the tomatoes are not very red.

- ❑ Add the wine, bay leaf, chopped parsley, salt and pepper. Cook on a low heat with a lid on, stirring occasionally, for 45 minutes. It should be quite dry by then.

- ❑ Meanwhile prepare the bechamel sauce. First heat the milk to just below boiling point.

- ❑ Melt the butter in another saucepan, add the flour and stir for a few moments over the heat to cook. When the roux changes consistency, remove the pan from the heat. Gradually add the hot milk, stirring well to avoid lumps. Bring to the boil, stir and reduce the heat, then continue to cook for a few minutes more.

- ❑ Add 50g grated kefalotiri to the sauce and season with nutmeg, salt and white pepper. The sauce should be neither too thin nor too thick.

- ❏ Remove bechamel from the heat and allow to cool. When it is completely cold, beat in the egg.

- ❏ Cook the pasta in a large pan of boiling salted water until *al dente* (about 7 mins). Drain well in a colander.

- ❏ Put half the pasta into a large, rectangular, ovenproof dish and sprinkle with half the remaining grated kefalotiri. Season with salt and pepper.

- ❏ Remove the bay leaf from the meat sauce and pour sauce over the pasta. Pile remaining pasta on top and sprinkle with the remaining cheese and a little salt and pepper.

- ❏ Finally pour the bechamel sauce over the pasta and bake for 30 minutes at 180°C/Gas 4, or until the top has a nice golden colour.

Katelios Taverna

Katelios is a small fishing village and fledgeling resort in the south of the island, a few miles from Skala. It has a reputation locally as one of the places to go for good fresh fish. The family-run Katelios Taverna on the waterfront specialises in fresh fish, live lobster and Greek cuisine. They also make a very good pastitsio!

Unable to find 'pastitsio pasta', I test drove this recipe with macaroni, but you could also use a small Italian penne which should be easier to find in the UK. I also had to substitute strong cheddar for kefalotiri - it was still quite delicious and there's one in the freezer for another day. - Ed

The Lost Canal of Xerxes *by Michael Looker*

- Herodotus Vindicated

In 486 BC Darius I, king of Persia, died and was succeeded by his son Xerxes (c519-465 BC). After resolving problems closer to home with Egypt, Xerxes set out to subdue the Greek states that had given his father so much trouble and eventual defeat at Marathon in 490 BC.

Contributing to his father's problems had been the destruction of General Mardonius' fleet when sailing around the Mount Athos Peninsular in treacherous stormy seas. Although the Athos peninsular (the eastern finger of modern day Halkidiki) rises to a great height, the place where it joins the mainland is and was a low lying, almost level area, just 2 kms from coast to coast. With forward planning, Xerxes had a canal dug across the neck of the Mount Athos peninsular, to avoid a similar fiasco.

Herodotus, a well respected Greek historian (c484-425 BC), states that the canal was about 2 km long and wide enough for two war triremes to pass through side by side. He described how it was dug in sections by men of different nationalities from Xerxes armies, taking three years to complete (483-480 BC).

It must have been as much a feat of labour management as of engineering. As each group cut their section of the trench at the prescribed width, the soil would be passed up in baskets through a chain of workers, to be dumped by those at the top. Inevitably where they cut vertically, the sides kept falling inwards, increasing the effort needed. Herodotus reported that the Phoenicians were the most skilful and did not make this mistake. They started digging across an area twice the prescribed width, gradually sloping inwards, so at the necessary depth they had a trench the same width as their fellow teams.

Artachaees was in charge of the construction works - a man Xerxes had great respect for. He was said to be the biggest and loudest man in Persia, but sadly he fell sick and died whilst Xerxes was in the area before the canal was finally completed. Xerxes had him buried with much ceremony and the army raised a high mound over his grave - there was plenty of freshly dug soil available!

After passing through the canal, Xerxes' army fought their way down into Greece, via the famous battle at Thermopylae in 480

BC (where the Spartans made their futile but heroic stand), and went on to sack Athens.

Since those times there had been no sign of the canal and doubt was cast on the reliability of Herodotus. A later source said that the route at the southern end of the supposed canal was obstructed by hills and that solid rock made digging impossible. It would indeed have been a massive undertaking in 5th century BC Greece, without the use of pulleys.

Since 1992 a team of British and Greek scientists and archaeologists have been investigating the area using a variety of techniques now available, including seismic survey and the drilling of bore holes. Seismic refraction and reflection measurements provide decisive evidence for the existence of the canal with dimensions that tally with those described by Herodotus!

The northern end of the canal has been defined (near to modern day Nea Roda) with less certainty than the centre of the canal, but the southern route has not yet been determined, although boreholes have confirmed that the ground was workable so earlier arguments suggesting the canal was impossible are invalid. Historians have speculated for

Picture from Hellenic Mapping & Cadastral Organisation

some years that the hill by the southern canal entrance is the burial mound of Artachaees. Evidence from the analysis of sediment shows that after the passage of the Persian fleet, the canal quickly fell into disuse, silted up and disappeared.

And anyway - it didn't do Xerxes much good - his fleet was defeated at Salamis later in the same year and in the next (479 BC) his army suffered the same fate at Plataea. The hapless Xerxes retreated back to Persia, and was later assassinated in 465 BC.

Details confirmed with Dr V. K. Karastathis, Senior Researcher, Prof. Stavros Papamarinopoulos & Dr R. E. Jones, archaeologist.

Lucian of Samosata *by Terry Cook*

- Don't Believe Everything You Read ...

For those brought up in the 'early days' of television - you know, when there were only two or three channels to choose from, and colour was something reserved for paint tins - satire was a novel concept the uninformed mind thought was invented by the new fangled box, ever seeking new and exciting things to bring 'entertainment' into the home.

So much for education - David Frost, Peter Cook, and a long line since them, are but novices in the art of poking fun in a serious way at the stupidities of the world around us and the people who claim to know what's going on. Back in the 2nd century AD, Lucian, born in southern Turkey (then part of the Syrian province of the Roman Empire), educated in Greek Ionia and widely travelled throughout the Roman-Greek world, is credited with popularising comic satire as not only an art form, but a serious attempt to establish a grasp on reality in a world he saw as fast losing its grip on what was important. Familiar scenario ?

No doubt a bit of a dreamer in his youth, his parents decided he should learn a trade and make an honest living with his uncle - a reputable sculptor - but working with marble proved not to be one of his better skills. On his first day he recounts, his chisel slipped and broke an expensive slab in two, thus provoking his uncle's wrath and his swift departure from the world of manual labour.

He goes on to justify his future calling by telling how he then dreamt that two women - one masculine in appearance like a workman, the other having a lovely face and fine figure, representing Culture - were fighting violently over who should have him. How much of the dream was 'real' and how much his elaborate excuse for going his own way we cannot tell, but he set about a life of learning, aided and funded by his ample capability to tell a good story. Thus as a lawyer and rhetorician he travelled throughout the Roman Empire pleading cases, making speeches and educating the masses.

By middle-age he'd either tired of this or made enough capital to settle down in Athens where he began a prolific writing career. A brief spell in the civil service in Egypt, to bolster his earnings or just give him a diversion, broadened his outlook and source for material even further, but he returned to his adopted Greece, and died in Athens somewhere between the ages of 60 and 80. A mediaeval account says he was torn apart by dogs, but this is believed to be a fabrication by the Church to denigrate his strong critique of Christianity.

His works poked fun at the ludicrous things he saw around him, or exposed charlatans whom he considered were duping the populous with their ridiculous theories.

He wrote a treatise on how to write history in which he emphasised again and again that 'the true facts' were the only criteria, but if your account was also entertaining and enjoyable, that was a bonus. Then to prove his point about the many false histories around, he wrote 'A True History' largely parodying Homer's Odyssey, in which are many outlandish stories including a trip to the moon! Credited with saying that the only guaranteed truth was that the whole thing was a complete pack of lies, he has influenced many great authors through the ages, notably Erasmus, Thomas More, Cerano de Bergerac, Jonathan Swift, William Shakespeare and Jules Verne.

Writing sometimes as dialogues and sometimes as observations, his insight and wit were combined with an excellent command of the Greek lan-

guage, despite his childhood tongue being Aramaic. He always managed to keep a perspective on reality. As Simon Goldhill wrote in his work on the cultural history of Hellenism, *"undercutting his success by inserting the audience reaction, he saves himself from believing in himself, and spares himself the humiliation of his reader's derision by being there first with the joke."*

Not exactly in the mould of modern-day 'grumpy old men' just fed up with modern attitudes and trends, he actually promoted a better understanding of life. How much he was listened to in second century Athens and how much he would be regarded for his wisdom today is something only historians could record - if you can believe what they say!

Research inspired by reading 'Lucian Selected Dialogues' see book reviews p167.

Peloponnese Castles 1686-1715 *by Peter Greaves*

What attracts me to castles is their sheer size and the freedom to wander about in them. In my early days of exploration the sites were unkempt, unsupervised and free which contrasted with the manicured, regulated and 'charged for' situation prevailing in Britain. There were no gravel paths nor closely mown lawns with notices about keeping off the walls or 'Beware of falling masonry'. These latter notices would have been more relevant in Greece as would some advice on how to avoid the wildlife (specifically snakes) harboured in the undisturbed vegetation.

My interest was informed by the three volume paperback series 'Fortresses and Castles of Greece' by Alexander Paradissis (publisher Efstathiadis), which gave a comprehensive and learned view of all the extant castles with a description and a little history. Since those early days some of the castles have been taken in hand and now have official opening hours (usually 8-2 and 6 till sunset) and even glossy well translated guidebooks available.

For this article I have concentrated on some of the 13 castles retaken by the Venetian Doge Francesio Morosini in his campaign 1686-1690 to reclaim the Peloponnese, but lost again to the Turks in 1715. It was during this campaign that the Parthenon was damaged when ammunition stored there was ignited. Pictures of all these castles are shown as a border round the 1684 map of the Peloponnese by the Dutch Geographer F de Witt.

Neokastro at the south end of Navarino bay (west coast), overlooks Pylos (Πύλος) and, as its name indicates, there is an old 'kastro' nearby. **Paleokastro** is at the north end of Navarino bay, perched high and isolated on the slope above the wildlife salt marsh lagoon of Gialova. Built in 1207 this castle is on a super site and well worth the 20 minute hike up the hill

beyond Nestor's cave, knowing that the sandy bay (mentioned by Homer) is available to swim in after your exertions. There is a barbican entrance and there are surviving curtain walls, ruins and wells inside.

Back to **Neokastro** which was built by the Turks in 1573 to control access to the safe anchorage of Navarino Bay after their naval defeat at Lepanto in 1572. The northern entrance to the bay was obstructed with a chain, making Paleokastro redundant. Neokastro was built with the best military engineering techniques. It encompassed 7.5 hectares, enough for a small town or to shelter the population of a wide area inside its 8 metre high walls, 2.5 metres thick, reinforced with bastion towers and angled to deflect incoming artillery. The ramped accesses were designed for the deployment of 69 cannon on two levels. There is a large internal citadel part of the walls adjoining the original main entrance from the land. This had three cisterns for collecting rainwater, slightly more secure than the one kilometre aqueduct which brought water to the main castle area. The design strategy betrays the fear of attack from the sea rather than the land. The capture of the castle in 1686 by Morosini, who landed troops and laid siege for only 12 days, showed its weakness.

The Turks reoccupied in 1715, but it was another sea battle in 1827 (when the combined Anglo-French-Russian fleets defeated the Turkish-Egyptian fleet in Navarino and guaranteed Greek success in their War of Independence) that resulted in its abandonment as a military installation, apart from some evidence of anti aircraft installations during World War II. For those who like the long view it is worth remembering that Navarino was the first ever defeat for the previously invincible Spartans in the Peloponnesian War against the Athenians. It broke the myth of their invincibility. Finally, a little known fact, Navarino is named after the company of mercenary soldiers from Navarre (Spain) who succeeded the Franks in the Peloponnese in the chaos of the Crusades.

Further down the coast on a peninsula at sea level is one of the 'eyes of Venice' at **Methoni** (Μεθώνη). Controlled from 1207 to 1500 by Venice then by the Turks until recaptured by Morosini in 1686 and held until 1715.

Methoni Moat

The structure is clearly Venetian with at least a dozen winged lions of St Mark carved into the stonework. The peninsula was utilised to create a moat on the landward side, now dry but crossed by an arched causeway. The curtain walls enclosed a town of 2,000 people making it the largest fortress in the Peloponnese. At its southern end is its most photographed feature, the **Bourtzi** (Μπούρτζι). This was an offshore strongpoint with an octagonal tower on two levels, connected by a causeway to the castle. The main citadel is at the opposite end.

Koroni (Κορώνη) castle, the other 'eye of Venice', is set high on a peninsula above the harbour it protects and has the same history as Methoni. It looks like an archetypal castle with an enormous barbican of rounded towers (one of which was damaged by the retreating Germans in 1944 when they ignited their arsenal inside). It has an extensive settlement inside with numerous churches, all char-

acteristically well kept with beautiful frescoes and fittings.

Monemvasia (Μονεμβασιά), the Gibraltar of Greece, is a rocky headland 300 metres above sea level with a 3 km perimeter. The name means 'single entry' which is over a man made causeway, now a tarmac road, but originally a 14-arched bridge with a central section of removable wood to aid security.

The flat plateau provided a good site for the citadel, cisterns for collecting rainwater, and the beautiful Ag. Sophia church perched above a rocky precipice. The first town was built up here and then extended to a lower town on the flat area at the base of the cliffs. The two were connected by a zig-zag path emerging from the warren of narrow streets. The lower town could not expand further and so built upwards thus increasing the sense of containment. Obviously there is no vehicular traffic beyond the causeway and this enhances the feeling of how things used to be. There has been much renovation in the lower town to provide accommodation and interest for visitors.

Its natural advantages mean that Monemvasia was only ever captured after long sieges which had to be from both the land and the sea. In 1540 it was surrendered to the Turks, along with Nafplion, without either being conquered, although it had endured a 3 year siege. It took Morosini 14 months to capture it in 1690.

Nafplion (Ναύπλιον), the first capital of independent Greece, is surmounted by the Fortress of **Palamidi** (Παλαμίδι) 216 metres above sea level. The fortress consists of a succession of eight self contained and independent bastions, 6 to 22 metres high, arranged so that succeeding towers could still enfilade (direct fire along a line) to and beyond the captured towers should they be taken. Offshore on a reef is another **Bourtzi**, built in 1471, as a strongpoint and to control the navigation of the Gulf.

When the Venetians captured the castle in 1687 Morosini strengthened the defences. When the Turks retook it in 1715 they constructed the internal high tower. A number of the bastions which surrounded Palamidi have been demolished to facilitate civic improvements so it is less easy to get a feel for the complete defensive works. However the Xenia hotel is on the site of one of these bastions and staying there does remove a lot of the uphill walk to explore Palamidi. Incidentally it was named after Palamides of Nafplio, who invented the lighthouse, the art of navigation and measuring scales, but was killed in Troy by his fellow Greeks on a false charge of treachery brought by Odysseus.

I urge you, if you are near one of these sites, to spend an hour or so visiting the massive structures erected before Morosini's campaign and still very impressive today.

Ancient & Modern *by Judith Hepper*

I managed Mycenae a little better this year. On our last visit I was overwhelmed by the looming Cyclopean masonry and the daunting prospect of entering the great Lion Gate. As I sat like 'the watchman on the walls' at the opening of Aeschylus' play about Agamemnon's return to his palace, my imagination forced me to hear the din of battle, the screams of betrayal, the choking of murderous death. So, on this year's Damaris expedition, I lingered in the museum and focused on the grave goods with their safely domestic objects: a clay sieve, drinking vessels, storage jars, vases and rings. Such familiar things reminded me of the everyday life of many of the people who lived within the citadel, and indeed of my own life at home in England, and I almost took Mycenae in my stride.

We were reminded again of the similarities between those ancient times and our own when, two days later, we visited the site of Nestor's Palace very early in the morning. The low sun shone through gnarled olive trees. The dew still sparkled on the petals of sweet-scented roses in the garden, which was full of birdsong. Everyone moved quietly around the few remains of this once-magnificent complex, built originally of wood, on silty sand, and therefore sadly ephemeral. The archaeologists who unearthed the sacred hearthstone and the deep stone bath also found thousands of terracotta vessels. Nestor, who commanded his fleet of ninety black ships to wrest Helen back from Troy, was a wise and hospitable ruler, who loved to entertain his people. His precariously-balanced piles of cups and jugs and bowls in the beautiful museum at nearby Hora looked exactly like the contents of our own kitchen cupboards, we all agreed. We were fortunate, on our trip, to meet with similar hospitality. The mother of Christos, our driver, is held in great affection by regulars in the group, and this year she made us delicious cheese pies to eat on the journey. In Athens, Christos entertained us at his favourite taverna. Mother came too, along with Konstantina his wife and baby Giorgios, and we danced the night away. On other occasions bunches of sweet grapes and juicy figs, bought in the local markets, were handed round the coach as we tried to emulate the warm hospitality of the Greek people.

Such links between old and new preoccupied me on this visit. We were delighted to have three opportunities for swimming this year: two in the sea, one in a hotel pool. Who could resist the water at the end of a day spent tramping round the sites, especially as at nearly every one we could gaze at the remains of the bathhouses and plunge pools, and marvel at the illustrations of the original decorative tiling, depicting leaping dolphins and nubile Nereids, around the baths? Then there were the enticing, clear, cold sacred springs (at Messene, for example, where Ithoma and Neda drew water to bathe the baby Zeus). Of course, when we swam we took off our protective layers of clothing, and one became aware of the human form: the marble-like roundedness of shoulders, the shadow in an underarm hollow, the mould of muscles in the thigh, the arch of a foot, all exactly as we had seen them portrayed in the marvellous statuary in every museum. Edward fell and cut his leg, on the shin where the taut skin is paper-thin. How well that tautness was depicted by the Greek sculptors and the artists who decorated the wealth of urns and votive offerings. How appropriate that we were on our way to Epidavros, the temple of Asklepios, the god of healing. (As the rituals required an overnight stay and close encounters with snakes, Edward turned instead to the local hospital, where the wound was stitched with speedy efficiency.)

So sculpted bodies became fascinating: the human form under drapery, for example, where a foot peeped or a knee protruded. In his own beautiful room in the museum at Delphi the Charioteer's hand curves with surprising delicacy to balance a rein in his upturned palm, and his little toes curl under in a startling piece of realism. In the museum at Olympia I was gazing at the figure of another charioteer, Myrtilos, part of the glorious east pediment from the temple of Zeus, with its narrative theme of the chariot race between Pelops and Oinomaos. He is represented as half-kneeling: there was the tautness of the stomach muscles, the stretched skin on the bent knee, the weight of the buttock as it balanced on the upright foot. I turned from my contemplation and saw one of our group crouching down to take a photograph. The stance was a complete replica of my statue, to an uncanny degree.

Photo by Sylvia Cook

Of course the statues represent our common humanity, particularly in depicting emotions: the joy and delight which we were sharing, but also pain, fear, passion, arrogance and lasciviousness. An actor with a challenging role to

play could well study the facial expressions of Greek sculptures to see exactly how the face muscles behave under the stress of strong emotion.

Luckily our tour proceeded sun-nily! We continued to find things that had resonance for us. In the elegantly restored Stoa museum in the Agora at Athens a fellow-grandmother beckoned me to see a really functional child's potty, with a helpful photograph nearby depicting a real baby wedged into

the frame which held the squalling infant in place above the receptacle. In the same museum I stood with an experienced magistrate to study a com-plicated grid of counters, a device for drawing lots for jury service. Close by was another method of casting votes: ostracism tablets, in this case univer-sally blackballing poor Themistocles. We felt for him.

Everybody in our group, however, had settled into easy camaraderie. It would be hard to leave the circle - but our arrival in Athens meant that the halcyon days would soon be over. It was time to think about what to take back for the family. I couldn't improve on my photograph of a wonderfully-moulded, muscular terracotta dolphin bounding over the waves for a dol-phin-loving child. More photographs, perhaps, to show the girls: an exqui-site bracelet from the seventh century BC (a snake to wind round your wrist, with a delicately-patterned head and tail), or the varied designs of ties and clasps to hold a dress, carved with exquisite attention to detail on the stat-ues at Nemea. The boys should be happy with their museum postcards of splendid horses competing in lion-hunts and chariot races or prancing to war. It is remarkable how little people's interests and preoccupations change in three thousand years!

So now it is time for leave-taking. Christos, John and the two Mikes must perform the thirteenth Labour of Herakles - heaving our suitcases onto the coach - for the last time. Our faces are nearly as sad as those we have seen on many a bronze relief: a warrior, turning as he bounds onto a stylish chariot to bid farewell to his wife, who stands disconsolately by with their baby in her arms, or, more poignant still, wives, sons and daughters grieving beside a figure departing to the afterlife. We are more fortunate, as we shall meet very soon at our reunion, to share memories and pictures and, no doubt, plan another trip. Meanwhile - home - and the pleasure of seeing again those curiously familiar objects (cooking pots and combs, beakers and bracelets) so remarkably similar to the artefacts made and used thousands of years ago, but no less useful, beautiful and cherished than our own.

Mythology

Ancient Greek Gods Alive and Well *by Terry Cook*

I'm one of many people disillusioned by religion, and concerned about the 'warring' of nations today under the justification of this god or that. But when I read of a recent upsurge in the worship of the ancient Greek gods, I was curious enough to want to know more. I had always put Zeus, Apollo, Athena and the other deities of ancient Athens in the 'outdated' category and ignorant belief in them as more mythology than reality.

But even Cavafy talks of the presence of the ancient gods in modern Greece:

> *That we've broken their statues,*
> *That we've driven them out of their temples,*
> *Doesn't mean at all that the gods are dead .....*

Around the world today there are a number of groups professing some form of belief in the Olympian gods - from Hellenic reconstructionism, which some brand as neo-paganism, to people like James Head who had a 'personal epiphany' during a day trip to Delphi nearly 20 years ago, and has been guiding interested followers ever since. For many years, such worship was an underground movement in Greece. Recently, however, one group based in Athens (called Ellinais) won a court battle for state recognition of the ancient Greek religion and has applied to register its offices as a place of worship.

Ceremonies are now being held in public - sometimes in defiance of Culture Ministry bans aimed at 'preserving' ancient sites. More and more people,

including the well-educated and some respected members of modern Athenian society, are coming out into the open to profess their discontent with modern organised religion, and joining what might appear to be bizarre rituals in a modern society. They don't go as far as animal sacrifice, however, deferring to the more symbolic and spiritual side of the ancients' worship, such as pouring wine as a libation to honour their chosen god. For some it is a re-awakening of spiritual and cultural awareness in an all too materialistic society.

from 'Ionic' from C P Cavafy: Collected Poems translated by Philip Sherrard and Edmund Keeley, published by Hogarth Press. Reprinted by permission of The Random House Group Ltd & Princeton University Press.

To quote Hellenion - a US-based group with adherents in many countries including Greece - "*Whatever the world may think of us and what we do, we know we are bravely moving forward with what we know to be right. We know that we are not gods, and need no reminding that we are merely human - but we are human! We have minds capable of compassion as well as research, wildness as well as reason, humour as well as piety. We are capable of understanding geometry, law, philosophy and art. We are capable of contemplating our own existence, its end, and questions of how one should live one's life in between. We respect one another's right to learn, think, and choose. But we come together, lending each voice in one chorus. Our diversity does not drive us apart, but adds to our perspective. Together we are more than we would ever be in separation.*"

These are fine words which could be echoed by any sane and thoughtful human being, so if a revival of bygone beliefs could achieve this, then why not?

Maybe pouring new wine in a special place as a libation to a god from bygone days is not what *you* might do with the fruits of the earth, but perhaps wearing robes and paying homage to the gods of old isn't really all that different from the 'worship' you see in any mainstream church today. And it does strike me as more forgiving and less confrontational of adherents to other faiths. So next time you're in Greece, don't be surprised if there's something going on in the local temple to Athena or Zeus. For now, I'll stick with Dionysos until I've cracked this 'spilling wine on the ground' business, while I can still remember where my mouth is !

Photo by Sylvia Cook

Are there 'closet' worshippers amongst this crowd?

So Who Does Pay the Ferryman? *by Terry Cook*

It is clear from the religion and myths of Ancient Greece to modern day that one thing man has never quite managed to understand is death. Following the trend of other eastern religious thought and practice, the Greeks endeavoured to explain in 'human' terminology what they could expect from living and from dying. The meaning of all things is explained through the complex cycles of the gods, their offspring and their escapades. So Erebus (a gloomy place between the earth and hades) and Nyx (the night or darkness) were both conceived from Chaos, the primeval emptiness of the universe before things came into being.

They in turn bore Charon, most often depicted as a sulky old man or winged

demon carrying a double hammer, who was the ferryman of the dead. When Hermes brought the souls of those no longer living, it was Charon's task to carry them across the dark rivers to the infernal regions beyond, and their eternal destiny. Cynically it should be noted that he actually had a nice little earner, some say that undertakers are the modern equivalent, and it could cost you dearly to depart this world in style! For Charon it was one *obol* - an ancient Greek coin worth about a sixth of a drachma - though occasionally he would accept a *danace*, a Persian coin worth considerably more.

There were five rivers separating the mortal world from that beyond, and most mythologists say it was Acheron (the stream of woefulness and sorrow) across which you needed the guidance of an expert. Others say it was the Styx which represented hatefulness and intense darkness, but this was more likely the place of one hundred years' purgatory where you were banished if Charon would not accept you on first arrival. If you did not have the fare (the ancients would place the coin beneath the tongue of the corpse upon burial if they could afford it) or if you had not had correct rites performed, you had to wait until due penance was done.

Charon was aided here by the fearful, three-headed dog Cerberus who would challenge any unauthorised spirits, though like most things, the Greeks had a way round this obstacle. Some honey cake would be buried with the body, and this apparently appealed to the hound's sweet tooth and kept him quiet and at bay. Of course, there were also several well-known back entrances which those wishing to avoid the ferryman's fee could use, if they could stand the noxious fumes which exhaled from the sulphurous fissures leading to the underworld.

In particular any living creature was positively discouraged from even trying to enter the 'lower' kingdom, and it took all of Hercules' powers of intimidation to get past the avaricious old man when, for one of his Labours, he was despatched to bring Cerberus back up to the land of the living. Orpheus, however, played an extremely enchanting melody on his lyre, and that persuaded Charon to row him over the darkness. Aeneas, on advice of the Cumaean Sibyl, used a golden bough to bribe his way to the underworld - a means adopted throughout the ages for many a difficult task or passage! But it was the dead to whom Charon's life work was dedicated.

Before their safe arrival in the kingdom of Hades and Persephone, the dead still faced the fiery river Phlegethon and the river of wailing and lamentation, the Cocytus, then they had to drink of the river Lethe - the waters of forgetfulness and oblivion (there's a Belgian beer similarly named 'Leffe' - possibly with the same effect!). Finally the three judges of the dead - Minos, Aeacus and Rhadamanthus - would assign each soul according to their just desserts.

The virtuous or heroic would be rewarded in the Elysian Fields with everything that was pleasant, peaceful and perfect happiness. The wrongdoers and evil would be sent to Tartarus where they would be eternally punished for their misdeeds. The bulk, however, symptomatic of the ancients' disillusionment with things spiritual, would be made to wander as dull shadows among the flowers of Asphodel which adorned the Elysian dream - able only to gaze on perfection.

Yes, it does all seem a bit far-fetched, but not so different from any of man's crazy beliefs about the meaning of life? In Lucian's day, 2nd c. AD Athens, there were obviously large numbers who took no heed of the Ferryman and what they must pay to cross safely to the other side. One of Lucian's satirical dialogues was between Hermes and Charon, the latter having persuaded the messenger god to show him everything man got up to before they were despatched to make use of his services. From a high point above Mt. Parnassus, Hermes showed him all the follies and fancies of the world.

After viewing all the effort, all the strife and all the pointlessness of man's existence, he declares *"What fools! ... what a troubled existence ill-starred humanity does have, with its kings and gold ingots and sacrifices and battles - and never giving a thought to Charon, the Ferryman they undoubtedly must one day pay."*

We may not have all the answers - but we can be sure that in life or death, the price must be paid to someone. What is it they say, *"There's no such thing as a free dinner"* or maybe (and I add this disclaimer for any or all of the details above), whatever you or I care to believe or not, we've heard it all before, somewhere.

Language Difficulties

Crossed Purposes *by Sylvia Cook*

We enjoy sitting amongst the hubbub of Greek voices outside Alekos' kafeneion, sipping our ouzo or wine. It's a bit like Greek music to our ears - no need to translate, just let the sounds wash over you and *be there*. Occasionally we pick out the odd word and think we know what they are talking about and we smile when they laugh, rarely understanding the joke. After a cloudy day cooped up working inside Spiti Cook, which followed four similar unusually cloudy and wet days in May, we were there one evening, appreciating the fresh if cool air outside.

There was the usual buzz of conversation and friendly argument alongside us. At a pause, Kostas asked us what we thought would happen tomorrow. We'd been checking the Aegean meteorological website for the island to see when the end to this unseasonal weather was predicted. Terry confidently replied (in Greek) that there may be more cloud in the morning, but brighter later.

Kostas looked confused, as did the others, *"No, the football. Who do you think will win - Liverpool or Milan?"*

We had no idea they were even playing, let alone that the match had been the subject of the Greek conversation alongside us.

'Green Beans' I Presume *from Sylvia Cook*

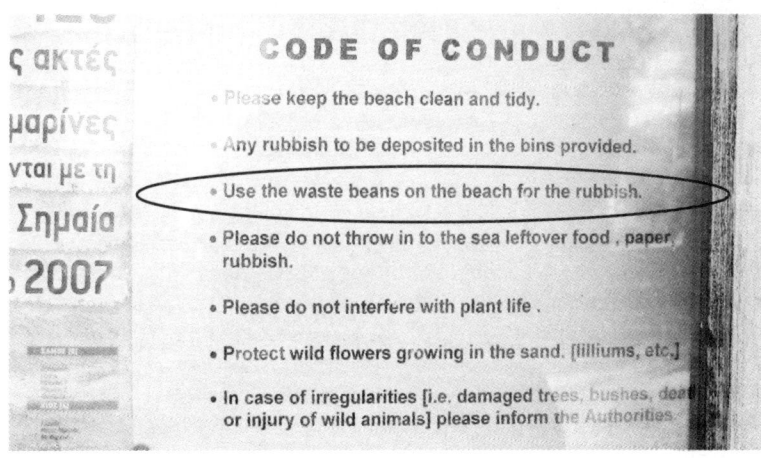

Law & Order *by Sylvia Cook*

Jean was just passing outside her friends' apartment in Skala Eresos and noticed the front door was wide open. Thinking this strange as they were visiting the UK, she went to investigate and was horrified to see the room stripped of their new wide-screen TV and other bits and bobs AND with graffiti written in large Greek letters over one wall. Immediately she contacted the local police who arrived in less than 3 minutes. 'Breaking and entering' for theft is thankfully a rare occurrence in this part of Greece.

Imagine her embarrasment when they translated the 'graffiti' to her. *"Do not put the tiles here."*

The workman employed while her friends were away had just popped out for a coffee, leaving the door open and the message (not to block his working area) in case an expected delivery arrived. Before starting on the work he had moved the new TV and other bits and pieces to another room!

Which Way? *from Sylvia Hodges*

Spotted in Skala, Kefalonia

Two Cretan Signs
from Alan Huff

Can't help wondering about a taverna encouraging customers in 'enjoinment' on the beach - Ed.

This establishment seemed a bit dodgy too - until I realised the name was in Greek letters - Ed.

Do You Think the Food is 'Ruff' in Here? *from Kath Riddell*

Culture

A Philhellene Welsh Poet *by Fr. Anastasios D. Salapatas*

Background

Let me tell you about Euros Bowen - a long story, but I shall try to cut it short.

In 1993 I came in contact with Euros' poetry. It seems I was the first Greek to discover him. A new book had just come out containing Euros' poetry in both Welsh and English (Euros Bowen, Priest - Poet, edited by Cynthia and Saunders Davies). I made contact with the translator (from Welsh into English) as well as with the editors. I expressed the desire to translate him into Greek. His family was also asked. Everybody was very happy with me working on Euros' poetry and translating his poems into Greek - so I did.

I published a long article on Euros and his poetry, with my translations of some of his poems, in one of Greece's best philosophical publications, called SYNAXIS. It really had an excellent reception. My article has even been quoted by many other Greek writers of poetic works. I am hoping to be able to work a bit more extensively on Euros in the future, when I find time.

Euros Bowen - The poet and his work

Euros Bowen was born in Treorci in South Wales in 1904. The place he was born and brought up is very well known for its coal mines and its great contribution to the British Industrial Revolution and Development. His father was a protestant pastor who greatly influenced Euros' future life and philosophy. He decided to study Theology in various Welsh Colleges as well as in Oxford. During his studies he became a member of the Anglican Communion and eventually he was ordained a Priest. He had served the same Parish (Llangywair with Llanuwchllyn) almost for the whole of his pastoral life and he didn't like moving out of his Parish, not even for holidays. After his retirement he moved to Wrexham, where he remained until his death in 1988.

When he retired he became a completely different person. He started touring around Europe, always on his own, as his wife didn't like travelling. He particularly liked to travel near the Mediterranean, looking around the archaeological and Byzantine sites, which he found in abundance in Greece, Cyprus, Constantinople, Asia Minor and the Greater Hellas (south Italy and Sicily). By going around, seeing and talking to people in the Greek lands, Euros was greatly inspired. He bore all the intellectual and cultural richness as well as the spiritual virtue of the Celtic people, which together with his Christian identity and commitment, he could transform into poetry baring all his inner feelings and moods. His poetic words are full of inspiration and sincerity, clear impressions and enthusiasm.

The language that he originally used in his poetry was his mother tongue,

Welsh. This ancient Celtic language is evidently poetic and certainly has the ability of expressing high thoughts in a special way. The poet himself had translated part of his poetry into English, in order to share with the international readership the essence of his wisdom and inspiration.

Euros Bowen is regarded as the greatest modern Welsh-speaking poet. He won many Welsh prizes for his literary contribution and published 14 volumes of poetry, as well as other works and translations.

Bowen's poetry is filled with classical Hellenic elements. One of his poetic collections (actually a complete book) is devoted to the Minoan civilisation. In most of his other published works we find whole poems, sentences and various words referring to the classical Hellenic spirit.

The poet is clearly inspired by this culture and is trying to make his interest and his respect well known. Thus, he presents in his own dynamic way, the spiritual feeling and the cultural vibration that he had felt by approaching the soil and the stones, the legends and the visions, the creativity and the literary and artistic production of an ancient people, which is still alive and thriving even today, as an invincible symbol of immortality and beauty.

Two of his most characteristic poems on classical Hellenic themes are presented here. Bowen himself comments on the first one entitled 'Mycenae': *"The original is written in free 'cynghanedd'. The sun at the height of summer at this famous site in southern Greece and the fort's ancient history of wealth and royal murders constitute a pattern of gold and blood".* (Poems reproduced with permission, translation of Mycenae by Fr. Salapatas)

MYCENAE

No grass allured,
    no passion there,
except for the gold of the sun
    spreading now
in the azure of day
and the passage of its blood
along the crest
    heavily
patterned with history
    over the stony ground,

Gold and blood
older
    than the oils of the
    gnarled olive-trees,

MYKHNAI

Ούτε χλόη σαγηνεύθηκε,
    ούτε πάθος εκεί,
εκτός απ' το χρυσό του ήλιου
    που απλώνεται τώρα
στη ζαφειρένια ημέρα
κι αιματοβάφει
το οικόσημο
    βαρύ
αχνάρι της ιστορίας
    πάνω στο πέτρινο έδαφος,

Χρυσάφι και αίμα
πιο παλιά
    από το λάδι των
    ροζιασμένων λιόδεντρων,

Gold and blood
younger than death
    in the guise of oblivion,
	Χρυσάφι και αίμα
	πιο νέα από το θάνατο
	    μασκαρεμένο σε λήθη,

Gold and blood
more fearsome
than the guardian arms
of all the compact woe
    of the bare cairn
within the Gates of Lions,
	Χρυσάφι και αίμα
	πιο τρομακτικά
	απ' των φρουρών την αρματωσιά
	της μαζικής συμφοράς
	    του ερειπωμένου τύμβου
	μέσα από τις Πύλες των Λεόντων,

Gold and blood
    of greater power
than the face-masks
binding the ascent
of the fossil speech
    of cellared bodies,
	Χρυσάφι και αίμα
	    ισχυρότερα
	από τα προσωπεία
	που φράζουν τη λαλιά
	του απολιθωμένου λόγου
	    των καταχωμένων σωμάτων,

Gold and blood
more famished
    in that place
than the step and gesture
of Agamemnon's nostalgic hour,
	Χρυσάφι και αίμα
	πιο πεινασμένα
	    στον τόπο εκείνο
	απ' το βήμα και την χειρονομία
	της νοσταλγικής του Αγαμέμνονα ώρας,

Gold and blood
a greater thirst
than the wrath
    that quickens the seed
of Clytemnestra's dark fever,
	Χρυσάφι και αίμα
	μια μεγαλύτερη δίψα
	κι απ' την οργή
	    που ζωντανεύει τον σπόρο
	του ζοφερού της Κλυταιμνήστρας πυρετού

Gold and blood of violent destiny in a place where no passion stirs, where no grass is allured.	Χρυσάφι και αίμα ανελέητης μοίρας σ' ένα τόπο όπου πάθος δεν εγείρεται, όπου χλόν δεν σαγηνεύεται.

The second poem takes us to Crete. The poet has again written a short comment: *"To the left of the road from Herakleion to Phaestos the mountain ridge overlooking the plain of Mesara forms a picture which is said to be the face of Zeus".*

Mount Iuktas (Ο.Γιουχτας), Crete - the face of Zeus from www.matrixofcreation.co.uk

ON THIS MOUNTAIN

Seeing is believing, so they say,
and here was seeing in the haze of this mountain,
between the restorations of Knossos
and Phaestos and its centuries,
the inheritor of the gifts of heaven and earth -
Zeus, from his concealing at birth in Dicti's cave,
and his nursing then in the cave of Idi,
at last setting his image
here in this earth, so they say,
in the mystery of the Isle of Crete.

Not everyone believes like Nietzsche
that God is dead,
because seeing is believing,
and so God himself is seen,
his forehead, his nose, his beard
lying on the mountain's ridge,
the picture unmistakably above,
with its glance over all the fruitfulness
of the plain of Mesara
acknowledging the earth as his possession,
the lemons, the oranges and the tangerines,
the strip's vines and the fecund olive trees.

Those who have tasted Bowen's poetic talent remain for ever admirers of his excellent way of looking at our world. He has been an outstanding representative of Welsh literary heritage, who has opened his vision to the Hellenic and other civilisations and by doing that he has produced an extraordinary kind of work, which has now become part of the universal poetic legacy.

Book Reviews

Reviews by Sylvia Cook (except where indicated)

The Long Shadow by Loretta Proctor

Publisher: Publish America, ISBN: 978 14241 01092, £15.50 (p/b 426p)

A teenage boy finds his mother's secret diaries which tell the story of her time as a Red Cross nurse in Salonica during the First World War and her tragic love affair with a Greek officer, his real father. In the second part of the story Andrew goes to Greece as a young man to trace his roots. He finds another side to himself through the music, dance and people he meets.

Movingly and vividly written by Loretta Proctor, herself an Anglo-Greek, The Long Shadow is an insight to medical and war conditions and the political confusion in Greece during WWI, but mostly a gentle love story and a tale of a boy growing up and reconciling his two cultural influences.

Lion of Macedon by David Gemmell

Publisher: Random House, ISBN 978 03454853 59, £7.99, €8.90 (p/b 514p)

Primarily a writer of heroic fantasy novels, David Gemmell has researched Greek history to create this triumphant novel about a fictional character, Parmenion, set in a period when Sparta was strong and culminating with the birth of Alexander. Being of 'mixed blood' the young Parmenion learns to fight for his life every day, becoming a great war strategist and general who assists Philip of Macedon. In the background a seeress tries to shape and steer his fate and that of Greece.

The Holiday by Erica James

Publisher: Orion Fiction, ISBN 978 07528433 08, £6.99 (p/b 528p)

An art teacher coming to terms with the end of a previous romance and a problematic relationship with her mother is invited to stay with friends in north east Corfu. They encourage a holiday 'fling' with their irresistible Greek neighbour, but does Izzy fall for him? Erica James builds her characters with humour and warmth, introducing sub plots and a touch of suspense. In romantic fiction tradition, they all live happily ever after.

To Watch the Waves Go By by Peter Stoneley

Publisher: BookSurge, ISBN 978 14196348 40, Amazon.co.uk from appr £8+ P&P, or www.PeterStoneley-OnCorfu.co.uk (p/b 245p)

Previewed in Vol 5 'Village Shopping - The First Time' regular Greek-o-Filer, Peter's book is now available. His 'memoirs' are an entertaining and colourful account of the ups and downs of planning and building a holiday home and making friends within a Greek rural community over 30 years. 'To watch the waves go by' will be enjoyed by all who dream of living in rural Greece or those who just love Greek ways. Peter and his wife were not to know when they bought their plot in the sun that the nearby beach village would become a centre for the worst kind of tourism. Their own experiences with local people just a short distance away could not be more different. (As a PS, read how Greek doctors saved Peter's life - p16)

The Papas and the Englishman by Roy Hounsell

Publisher: Yiannis Books, ISBN 978 0954788735, £7.99 (p/b 224p)

An unexpected redundancy and a chance to help friends in Corfu lead Roy and Effi (via pool and property maintenance in Corfu) to their dream home and life in an inland Zagorian village, next door to the local Papas. Roy's writing style and descriptions of people, events and the scenery in this unspoilt region of Greece make his book more than just an enjoyable relocation tale - it's an enticing invitation to visit and share the magic of Zagoria.

Poison in Athens by Margaret Doody

Publisher: ISBN 978 00994683 32, £6.99, €10.99 (p/b 480p)

Set in the autumn of 330BC this is the 4th 'Aristotle Detective' novel, my first. It took a while to get into, setting the scene at Aristotle's Lyceum and discussing how Athens was run at that time, but I soon got involved in the three law cases - a murder by hemlock, ownership of a beautiful slave-girl and an accusation of impiety - in which our raconteur and friend of Aristotle finds himself embroiled. It's a good detective story with all the intrigue and mystery of a modern 'whodunnit' with a history lesson thrown in for free.

The Athenian Murders by Jose Carlos Somoza

Publisher: Abacus, ISBN 978 03491161 81, £7.99, €10.35 in Greece (p/b 316p)

I bought this expecting an alternative to the Margaret Doody detective novel with Plato instead of Aristotle. At first awkward, the main story is an investigation by Heracles 'Decipher of Enigmas' into a series of murders in Ancient Athens, underpinned with translator's notes creating a second linked story. Philosophical ideas and a literary theme develop alongside the detective story and insight to ancient cults in Athens. The intriguing twist at the end explains all!

The Greek Taverna Cookbook by Gill Tomlinson

Publisher: Blue Shutter Press, ISBN 978 09554696 02, €24.05 inc UK p&p from www.artistswindow.com, or £14.99 direct Tel UK 020 3004 2617, (128p)

A beautifully and clearly presented collection of recipes assembled by Gill from recipes donated by her favourite and most appealing tavernas on Kefalonia. This spiral bound book includes 41 recipes and much more. Background information on local specialities and Greek food, taverna descriptions and locations, with Gill's own delightful paintings of each taverna plus small evocative illustrations to make you yearn to be sampling these dishes on Kefalonia. When you can't be there, you'll just have to follow the recipes and recreate the experience at home. *(see p140)*

Words of Mercury by Patrick Leigh Fermor

Publisher: John Murray, ISBN 978 07195610 61, £7.99 (p/b 274p)

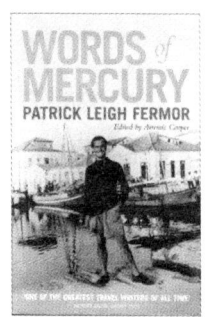

This anthology of extracts published in 2003 brings out the richness of Paddy Leigh Fermor's writings which reviewers have already extolled. It satisfies those with a voracious appetite for his work and reveals new titbits to discover and enjoy, whilst also presenting an insight to his extraordinary life on his journey to and then his exploits in Greece. His depth and style clearly portray his unmistakable talent both to tell a good tale and to faithfully depict those who have been part of his rich and colourful life. **Terry Cook**

Lucian Selected Dialogues by CDN Costa

Publisher: Oxford University Press, ISBN 978 01928059 35, £7.99 (p/b 286p)

A highly readable translation of the Greek texts with an introduction that puts Lucian in perspective and context. This well-chosen cross section of some of his best satire and comic dialogue is far more modern than its 2nd century AD pedigree would lead you to believe. If you thought Oxford World Classics meant dry and dusty tomes, then you'll be pleasantly surprised by how much of a good read this is. From the 'Praise of the Fly' to 'A True History' Lucian's 'brilliantly entertaining writing' also gives an insight to the thinking of his day that may surprise as well as educate. **Terry Cook**

The Collected Poems by C.P. Cavafy translations by Evangelos Sachperoglou

Publisher: Oxford University Press, ISBN 978 01992129 27, £9.99 (p/b 240p)

With Cavafy's undoubtedly unique place in Greek literature, and his perspective on the world summed up by E M Forster as 'a Greek gentleman in a straw hat, standing absolutely motionless at a slight angle to the universe', this collection of his work with new translation underlines just how perceptive he was in his poetry. The Introduction by Peter Mackridge, the parallel Greek and English texts, extensive chronologies and notes make this a worthwhile addition to the library of anyone interested in a view of life by one of the most important poets of the twentieth century. **Terry Cook**

Portrait of a Priestess by JB Connelly

Publisher: Princeton University Press, ISBN 978 06911274 60, £23.95 (h/b 456p)

Beautifully illustrated and presented, with exhaustive notes and bibliography, this is an excellent study into the role of women as priestesses from the highest to the lowest ranking. The author, from her vast experience in the fields of archaeology and fine art, demonstrates clearly how the role of women in religious office was more important than many believed. In conclusion she deals with how this subject affects our views today. **Terry Cook**

Around Greece in 80 Stays by Jacoline Vinke

Publisher: Road Editions, ISBN 978 608187 20, £25 (h/b 384p)

Feast your eyes on this beautifully presented weighty book and relish the descriptions of these wonderful stylish hotels and guesthouses of character on the mainland and islands. Not the cheapest places to stay, but certainly charismatic and not all outside the reach of the ordinary traveller who occasionally wants something special. It could provide inspiration for your own Greek home or guesthouse business too.

The Idiot & The Oddity by Tony Brown

Self published e-book, PDF available from www.grecofilia.co.uk, £2.95 (or CD by post direct from Tony, £3.65 Tel. 013 2628 0255)

In this e-book anti hero Godfrey arrives on Greek shores in the role of a modern day Odysseus. Appointed by fate, can he (as Odysseus before him) protect the heritage of a desperate people whilst the odds seem against them? Tony's tale weaves greed, lust, mythology and crime, together with family values, honour, music and a love and eye for all that is Greek. Throw in a Cruella de Ville-type ex-partner, a backdrop of blue Aegean sky, a shared secret, ancient relics and help from the goddess Athena and watch a story that starts off at a *'siga siga'* pace develop into a warp-speed crescendo as every good Greek drama should. In his first novel Tony Brown proves as ever to be a great observer of Greek life without reverting to caricature. **'SKLesvos'**

Prospero's Daughters by Sally Stewart

Publisher: Severn House, ISBN 978 07278631 95, £13.65 (h/b 224p)

Provided you are not seeking a literary masterpiece but just want a light novel with a Greek setting then this should fit the bill. It is the story of a young English woman who goes to Corfu to find out more about her grandfather who was killed in Greece in WW2. Her travels also take her to Athens and Delphi. It is unlikely I would have read the book had it not been set in Greece but it was a pleasant way to pass a few hours. **Jenny Booth**

Odysseus Unbound - The Search for Homer's Ithaca by Robert Bittlestone

Publisher: Cambridge University Press, ISBN 978 05218535 76, £30 (from £16 Amazon) h/b 598p

I was delighted to be asked to do some translation work for Robert Bittlestone to help in his research and thrilled to see my name mentioned in this brilliant and absorbing book. When I received my copy, I thought its content would be completely over my head (due to some difficulty in 'getting my head round' things scientific) - but how wrong I was! His relaxed, approachable writing style, geared to the non-academic reader; photographs and scientific images alongside beautiful descriptions and modern translations of excerpts from Homer's 'Odyssey'; the humour and infectious enthusiasm with which the whole thing is presented; all make for an extremely enjoyable read. 'Odysseus Unbound' has fired me with interest and great enthusiasm for a subject I knew very little about before. I can't wait for the next development in the search for Homer's Ithaca!

To demonstrate his style, this extract amused me. From Chapter 12 'Thinia' (having arrived in Kefalonia in 2003 to research) :

> *"So Melis, what do you do outside of the tourist season?"* We are being driven over the flank of Mount Ainos by Melis Antoniou, owner of the Greekstones car hire firm. ... *"I am well boring"*, he replied, demonstrating what we felt was an impressive grasp of teenage British argot coupled with an unexpected streak of humility previously unremarked in the Greek national persona.

> *"No, but really, there can't be enough tourists to run your business in the winter - how do you keep yourself busy?"* He wasn't being modest, he was being literal: he held one of the licences to bore water wells for the villagers on the island.

Melis later became involved with Bittlestone's research by providing his 'geological observations' about the area under scrutiny, made with a view to consider the drilling of boreholes to provide drinking water for the local people. The drinking water project was unsuccessful, as the underground water was found to be salty; giving strength to Bittlestone's theory that there was once a narrow sea channel between 'mainland' Kefalonia and ... Ithaca!

I translated an academic paper on the subject: 'Hypersaline Waters in an Enclosed Limestone Body of Kefalonia' written by Professor of Hydrogeology and Technical Geology, Ioannis Koumantakis!! Read the book to learn more.

Karen Rich

Musical Coals to Newcastle *by Collette Hurley*

I was lucky enough to spend a whole month in Greece this year, travelling on my own from Piraeus to the Cyclades islands on the wonderful Blue Star Ferry Boat and then between the smaller islands on the hardy little Skopelitis ferry.

Singing has been important to me as far back as I can remember and I have loved Greek songs ever since I first went to Greece in 1966.

Just over a year ago I helped to form a small Greek band (Ta Filia), along with a bouzouki player and a guitarist. We have played a number of gigs in and around our local Devon town and have made a demo disc with 5 tracks. Our repertoire to date includes Rebetika (the Greek blues) and popular songs by Theodorakis and Zographos.

My first musical encounter in Greece on my trip this year, was with a busker in Plaka, Athens, who was playing his bouzouki. He was sitting on a step outside an old building up near the Museum of Traditional Greek Musical Instruments. I spoke to him in my best Greek and asked him if he knew the song '*Strose to Stroma Sou*' (the one I am sure you will all recognise from Zorba the Greek), one of my very favourites. He knew it of course and we sang it there and then in harmony. That was a big thrill for me!

I showed the busker our demo disc and he wanted to buy it. My Greek wasn't good enough to explain that it was only a demo and not a full CD so he called over to a Belgian man he knew who lives on the street and who could speak good English. He translated and explained for me.

From Athens I travelled on to the island of Irakleia where my landlady, who spoke only Greek, became my friend very quickly. One day we went walking to pick vine leaves for making dolmades. As we walked we sang all the Greek songs that I know. She was amazed that I could sing in Greek.

One evening a group of Americans came into the harbour on a yacht with their Greek captain. We ended up all going out to eat together and in the taverna they played my demo disc. There are two instrumentals and three songs on it. The Americans all wanted a copy straight away and even the Greeks were complimentary about our efforts!

On Syros, my next stop, I sang a Greek song for my landlord there. He asked *"why?"* He really didn't understand why a foreigner would want to learn Greek songs. I tried to explain to him that it was a passion. He laughed and commented *"You're more Greek than me"*.

It was on the island of Folegandros that the demo disc was most appreciated. My Danish landlady there played it every morning at breakfast, which became a little embarrassing, as I wasn't the only guest there. Her Greek husband sang lots of new songs to me and we sang together sometimes.

The demo was played in two tavernas in the town and was very well received. There was a man who is a chanter in church who sang spontaneously as he sat drinking his coffee. I made a very short video clip of him with my mobile phone and then played it back to him which amused him very much. He and I sang *'Misurlu'* together - the song which Maria Farandouri made famous in Greece in the 1950s. It is a lovely poem written by Seferis and put to music by Theodorakis.

What struck me as sad was that live music and spontaneous dance is now such a rarity on the islands. Television has taken over, together with the ubiquitous mobile phone.

Folegandros has an annual festivities week in July and I was invited to return with 'our band' to play in the street next year, which is very exciting. I'm really looking forward to it and my fellow musicians are equally excited. We're still waiting for confirmation of details from the organisers, but can't wait to make our plans.

At the end of my month in Greece I went back to Athens for two nights. On the very last night I went to a taverna called Sisyphus where I sat and ordered wine and a meal. It was very quiet and only about 8.30pm. A bouzouki led trio was playing to an audience of about 5 tourists, including me. The two couples finished their meals and left and then it was just me and the band and the occasional waiter. I plucked up courage and walked up to the band, wine glass in hand and told them I sang Greek songs. The bouzouki player looked surprised and amused, the man on the drum looked a little alarmed and the guitarist just stared, but they indulged me and I sang - you've guessed - *Strose to Stroma Sou*!

I felt that I'd arrived then. I had fulfilled a dream - to sing with a bouzouki band in Plaka.

The band warmed to me and obviously liked my singing. Just then a group of Greek women arrived from a dance class, along with two belly dancers, one of whom was their teacher. The night really started to swing then and I was invited to join them at their table.

The belly dancing was spectacular and the dancers (both Americans) very friendly. We finished up at 1.30am drinking ouzo and eating with the band!

Meanwhile, back in the UK Ta Filia continue to play various gigs. Our latest one was terrific fun. A local pub put on a Greek night and filled the room with diners, one of whom got a bit too exuberant and smashed many plates, flinging them into the fireplace, with the landlord looking on indulgently! People danced and clapped and joined in with the choruses where they could.

Look out for us. We could be going places!

Here are the words of my favourite Greek song with English translation:

Στρώσε το Στρώμα Σου Για Δυό   Make Your Bed for Two

Ο δρόμος είναι σκοτεινός	The road is dark
ώς που να σ'ανταμώσω.	until I meet you.
Ξεπρόβαλε μεσοοστρατίς	Meet me in the road
το χέρι να σου δώσω.	that I may give you my hand.

- Ρεφραίν -	*- Refrain -*
Στρώσε το στρώμα σου για δυό	Make your bed for two
για σένα και για μένα,	for you and for me,
ν'αγκαλιαστούμε απ'την αρχή	that we may embrace each other from the start
να 'ναι όλα αναστημένα.	and all will be brought back to life.
- ν'αγκαλιαστούμε	*(repeat 3rd & 4th line)*

Σ'αγκάλιασα μ'αγκάλιασες.	I embraced you, you embraced me.
Μου πήρες και σου πήρα.	You took from me and I took from you.
Χάθηκα μες τα μάτια σου	I lost myself in your eyes
και στη δική σου μοίρα.	and in your fate.
- Ρεφραίν -	*- Refrain -*

(Greek from www.greekmidi.com/songs, translation from www.sacredcircles.com)

Greek Music Recommendations

Laki at Trehantiri has kindly come up with three varied recommendations for current CDs for our readers to add to their Greek music collections. Of course I asked for a suggestion to include Collette Hurley's favourite Theodorakis song with words, but also a traditional instrumental and a vocal mix.

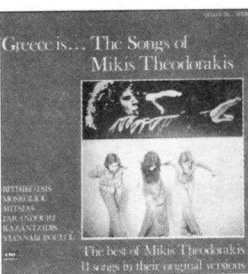

GREECE IS ...
The Songs of Mikis Theodorakis

Minos - EMI label , CD 045702272, £15.99

A selection of classic vocal tracks in the popular GREECE IS... series, sung by a variety of Greek artists including Gregoris Bithikotsis, Stelios Kazantzidis & Marinella duet, Maria Farandouri and more.

HELLAS GREEK MUSIC
Syrtaki - Hassapiko

Victory label, CD NOVM 30212, £15.99

A selection of classic Greek instrumental tracks to get you dancing, including amongst others: Siko Herepse Syrtaki, Horos Tou Zorba, Ta Pedia Tou Pirea, Frangosyriani, Oli I Rembetes. Ideal to get you in the Greek mood for a Greek party back home.

NON STOP MIX 3

Heaven Label, CD 5204958012329, £15.99

The latest medley compilation played throughout Greece and Cyprus in summer 2007, includes a wide variety of easy listening, Hassapika, Zeimbekika, Tsiftetelia and modern Greek pop music. Artists include : Despina Vandi, Panos Kalidis, Nino, Peggy Zina, Elli Kokkinou, Thanos Petrelis to name but a few.

Greek Quiz Answers *(Quiz on page 57)*

Sport
1. 776 BC
2. Just one race, the length of the stadium
3. 1896
4. 26 miles 385 yards (42.195 kms, distance run from Marathon to Athens)

Films
1. Stoupa, Peloponnese (they worked at a mine in nearby Pastrova)
2. Kefalonia (& UK)
3. Mykonos
4. Rhodes (studio shots at Elstree, Britain)

Geography
1. Less (Corfu av. 1097mm, London/Greenwich av. 584mm 1971-2000)
2. Mt Olympus / Mt Olymbos (2917m highest point)
3. 169 (source: Ministry of Press & Mass Media 1999)
4. Athos Peninsular, Halkidiki (Mt. Athos, or Holy Mountain)
5. Dodecanese Islands
6. Constantinople, now called Istanbul

History
1. A catastrophic volcanic eruption
2. Thermopylae
3. Cleopatra
4. The Ionian Islands (also known as the Septinsular Republic)
5. 1821
6. Lord Byron (died April 1824 of fever, whilst training Greek forces)
7. Rupert Brooke
8. Matapan (named after the southernmost cape of The Peloponnese)

Mythology
1. Jason
2. Heracles
3. Penelope
4. Schliemann
5. Delphi

General
1. The dregs left over from wine pressing, distilled & flavoured with aniseed
2. The kitchen table of Mon Repos which is now a casino on Corfu
3. Okhi Day (Όχι Μέρα)
4. Eleftherios Venizelos Airport

And Finally...

Promises Made and Broken *by Loretta Proctor*

- A wartime romance

My father, Alex Cairns, joined the RAF when he was eighteen years old, spending his twenty-first birthday on a troop ship bound for the North West Frontier in India. Here he served for six years before being sent on to Aden, then Malta. The Second World War broke out and my father was posted in 1940 with the Mediterranean Forces and sent to Athens.

As he was out on the town with a friend one day, he spotted a beautiful young woman walking along arm in arm with her own friends. They were a group of cheerful, young theatrical performers celebrating their latest success and singing as they walked along happily through Constitution Square. Alex fell in love in an instant. He said he knew she was his destiny there and then. He and his friend joined up with the group and both being fluent in French they began a conversation. During a drink at a nearby kafeneion Alex asked Diana Safralis to meet him again.

Now my father was as handsome as Diana was beautiful; she was attracted to him and agreed ... why not?... with a shrug of her slender shoulders. But she was a much courted and admired young actress and singer and having second thoughts (...a British airman, not even a commissioned officer!) so she didn't bother to turn up for the date.

However, my Dad was a persistent and crafty Geordie lad. He had followed her home when they parted after that first meeting and later arrived uninvited, knocking at her door, flowers spilling from his arms, full of Geordie charm, determined to win this glorious Greek goddess.

My mother was a trifle snooty in those days. She came from a comfortable and educated family with servants and a two storey house in an Athens suburb. So it wasn't as easy a courtship as he might have liked and he promised her all sorts of things. I do believe he meant to try and make them come true. Well, win her he did and they swiftly became engaged. The impending invasion of the Nazis hastened the wedding date and may well have played a part in my mother's sudden acceptance of marriage. I think

she may well have refused him otherwise. But this is hindsight and the outcome was that they married on Easter Day in 1941 at St. Paul's Anglican Church in Athens. The only flowers available were arum lilies as it was Easter. My superstitious mother has always felt white flowers to be bad luck since then.

At the reception a car arrived from HQ and my father and his best man were taken back to base. The Germans were marching from Salonika and the Forces had to withdraw with all speed to Crete. Diana, now a British citizen, claimed her passport at the British Embassy and was taken to the port of Piraeus. There were two boats waiting to evacuate the British civilians and with the wisdom of youth, she asked to go on the uncomfortable little ferry ship rather than the large elegant cruiser, Patrice 2. She felt instinctively that it would be less easy to spot. She was right for the larger ship was sunk while her smaller vessel made it to Souda Bay. She claims to this day that her miraculous ikon, packed in her little case, helped to save them all.

The soldiers went on into the mountains and forests to hide and she was the only woman amongst them. Diana recalls the officers sleeping in a ring around her to protect her from the Australian soldiers who, sadly, had a bad reputation in those days where women were concerned, though no-one denied their bravery in battle. She had a blanket above her and another below and it was very cold in those mountains.

Because Diana was Greek, she managed to get some eggs from a local farmer and made the officers an enormous omelette, much to their delight. They rolled back their collars and cuffs because they were so dirty and did their best to look smart when called to her tent for the repast.

Then she was taken over in a Sutherland aircraft to Egypt and Dad was allowed to come with her as they were newly wed. He sat at her feet in the plane, holding her hand. Thus they arrived safely in

Diana with Loretta in Egypt

Alexandria, Egypt. My father went off with his squadron and my mother stayed with her Auntie Emilia who lived there. Auntie had the unenviable task of using paraffin and a comb to get the lice out of Diana's hair! Later Diana managed to find a flat in Cairo and in that magical city I was destined to enter the world!

Sadly the marriage was never an easy one despite these romantic and exciting beginnings. My father arrived at the flat in Cairo one evening without shoes, without his cap, looking deranged and shocked. He had to be taken to a mental hospital. The strain of the war had suddenly taken its toll on his nervous system. He recovered but was never quite the same man again.

The marvellous life, the servants and fine house my naughty Dad promised were never likely to materialise in Newcastle, a city then so grimy, poor and undeveloped. My gran's dark, Victorian house in Scotswood Road and the bleakness of postwar Britain were an immense culture shock for my Greek mother who literally fainted from the cold snows of 1947, one of the worst winters of the century.

Immediately after the war, Mum had taken me over from Egypt to visit my grandmother in Athens, but that was the last we saw of her for many years. I was only to meet her again when she came briefly to England in my teens.

We lived the Forces life, moving from one married quarters to another until Dad at last retired from the RAF and we came to live in London. Life was poor and difficult and he fell ill once more, unable to cope with civilian life, succumbing to the manic-depression that haunted him until his early death at the age of 65.

However, Mum stuck faithfully and loyally to her unhappy marriage till Dad died in 1977 and their wartime love story ended forever.

Sometimes I wonder if my enduring love of writing romantic stories comes from my awareness of my parents' tragic love story. My debut novel, The Long Shadow, is set in Greece and has as a theme the conflict of a child who is born from parents of Greek and English nationality and the subsequent tension in that person's soul over where their roots lie and where their heart belongs. There must be many people in Britain of mixed backgrounds who face this dilemma nowadays and in the end I'm not sure there's a real conclusion ... but you'll have to read the book to see one possible solution!

(Loretta Proctor's book The Long Shadow is reviewed on page 164.)

THE BETTER PARTS OF GREECE

Both **Sunvil Holidays** & **The Greek Islands Club** have been specialists to Greece since the early 1970's.

Sunvil aims to give the seeker of the 'real' Greece a wide range of accommodation at reasonable cost on 21 quieter islands & lesser-known mainland areas.

The Greek Islands Club caters to those looking for peace and privacy, with a portfolio of exclusive villas in enviable locations, many with a pool.

Sunvil Holidays: 020 8568 4499 www.sunvil.co.uk (ATOL 808, AITO)

Greek Islands Club: 020 8232 9780 www.greekislandsclub.com (ATOL 848, AITO)

GREECE
satisfying so many desires

Stunning **Greek islands** and mainland **resorts**
Stylish properties & terrific choices for **families**
Private **taxi transfers** included
Superb **spa hotels** & **golfing** opportunities
Exclusive **wedding venues**

0871 871 2234
www.planet-holidays.net

ABTA W6455   ATOL 5998   AGTA

Planet Holidays

THE PAXOS SPECIALISTS

Self-catering village studios, apartments & country villas with pools

Tel: 01373 814200 www.planos.co.uk

 *Island Hopping Holidays*

Over 60 islands & 8 mainland destinations

enquiries@islandwandering.com 01634 868688
www.islandwandering.com

See also colour adverts front & back covers:

- Ionian & Aegean Holidays, Simpson Travel, Simply Travel, Flexi-cover Travel Insurance, London Greek National Travel Org.

Advertisers/Supporters - Travel Contacts

Lancashire Adult Learning

Greek Learning Breaks

Enjoy a relaxing and fulfilling break in the heart of Lancashire. Combine language classes with Greek themed social activities whilst enjoying all that Lancashire College has to offer, including excellent dining and residential facilities and good transport links.

- Fri 30/11/07 to Sun 02/12/07
- Fri 25/4/08 to Sun 27/04/08
- Fri 01/08/08 to Sun 03/08/08
- Fri 01/08/08 to Wed 06/08/08
- Sun 03/08/08 to Wed 06/08/08
- More dates to be confirmed

Please see www.lancashirecollege.com for more information.

For further details or to make a booking, call 0845 600 1331
Lancashire College, Southport Road, Chorley,
Lancashire, PR7 1NB
Email: insight@ed.lancscc.gov.uk

INVESTOR IN PEOPLE

Awarded for excellence

Modern Greek weekly classes: BEGINNERS to ADVANCED levels
Greek Saturday Immersion Day: 8 March 2008
THE BRASSHOUSE LANGUAGE CENTRE
50 Sheepcote Street, Birmingham B16 8AJ Tel:0121-303 0114 Fax:0121-303 4782
Email:brasshouse@birmingham.gov.uk Website:www.birmingham.gov.uk/brasshouse

---

@euroTalk.com
interactive language learning

HAVE FUN LEARNING GREEK!

Interactive language learning CD-ROMs

5 discs

Special Offer Price £49.99 (RRP £125)
FREE 100-Word Exercise Book
FREE post & packing
Quote ref: GG/GOF to receive this special offer **£49.99**
Tel: 0800 018 8838   www.eurotalk.com

Please tell advertisers you saw their details in **The Greek-o-File**. We rely on advertisers and try to find appropriate suppliers for our readers. They rely on respones to justify costs.

Greek Language Courses in Beautiful Kavala
To suit all levels. Groups of up to 5 people.
Tuition, accommodation & meals included.
www.grecophone.co.uk Tel: 01326 375161

Index

*In this index main article subjects are in **bold**, reference only items in plain text and place names are listed after their island or region name.*

Index

Index

The Greek-o-Files

If you have not read the first 5 volumes,
you can buy them direct from
Greek-o-File (or from some retail outlets)
to build your FILE on all things Greek.

Volume 1 ISBN 0-9543593-0-5 Ret £8.50
Volume 2 ISBN 0-9543593-1-3 Ret. £9.50
Volume 3 ISBN 0-9543593-2-1 Ret. £9.50
Volume 4 ISBN 0-9543593-3-X Ret. £9.50
Volume 5 ISBN 0-9543593-4-8 Ret. £10.50

DIRECT SUBSCRIBER OFFER
£6 per book
(includes UK post & packing)

All volumes are 192 pages, approx 50
illustrated articles in each book - all new
reader experiences, anecdotes and
researched articles from ourselves
and fellow Grecophiles.

Volume 6 and subsequent volumes **will NOT be reduced to £6** due to 'Print on demand' at higher unit cost.

(Details of content and extracts on website www.greekofile.co.uk)

Back Issues of former **Greek-o-File Quarterly Magazines** are also available - Autumn 1998 to June 2002, A4 prepunched pages build into a FILE of information and anecdotes. Four **Stock Clearance issues just £1** each, others at **£3 each** (inc UK p&p) or all **15** with a **FREE** white+logo 4-ring FILE & dividers for just **£35**.

Notecards - Sets of Images of Greece, Animals, Cats, Flowers, Lesvos or Eresos available. Watercolour impressions from photographs by Sylvia Cook. Each set has 9 cards 148 x 105mm with envelopes for **£4.20, 3 sets £11** inc VAT & UK P&P.

Greek-o-File Logos to personalise your T-shirt, sweatshirt, vest, shorts, sundress, or other cotton item - **Iron-on** Greek-o-File registered trade mark logos **cyan & black** (colour as book front) seagull silhouette & name, or just use the seagull, **3 logos 6x4cm** for **£1.95** or larger **2 logos 9x6cm** for **£2.50** inc VAT & UK P&P.

Greek-o-File™

Plus additional offers for direct subscribers.

Contact Greek-o-File +44 (0)1225 709907 or stc@greekofile.co.uk for latest information, or see website **www.greekofile.co.uk** for more details of books, magazines & notecards.

Reply Form

If you are not already a direct subscriber and would like to be **notified when future issues** are to be published, **order offer items**, or **send an article** for consideration in future books, please complete this form (or a copy) as appropriate and post with relevant additional details or payment to :

Greek-o-File, 29 Littlejohn Ave, Melksham, Wilts, SN12 7AW, UK

Name Mr/Mrs/Ms/Miss_____

Address_____

_____Post Code _____

Tel (Day / Eve)_____

Email address _____

Where did you buy/find this book? _____

I would like:

To be notified when future Greek-o-File volumes will be available   ___
If you purchased this book direct you will automatically be notified - let us know if you move.

Circle or underline as appropriate or send separate letter where clarification is needed.
Prices quoted **inc UK P&P** on all items and **UK VAT** on logos and notecards.

To purchase more Greek-o-File Paperback Books

Set of **all 6** books **£39** ___ or Vol 6 for **£9.50,** just **£6** each for other volumes   ___

Specify number & which volumes required _____

(For overseas postage add per book: Rest of Europe £1.20, Rest of World £2.50)

To purchase ALL 15 Greek-o-File loose leaf magazine back issues @ £35 ___
includes UK P&P AND a **FREE Greek-o-'File'** (4-ring A4 white file with dividers).

Individual issues available @ **£3** each, four stock clearance @ **£1** each.

To purchase Greek-o-File Notecards   1 set of 9 for **£4.20**,   3 sets **£11**   ___
- specify sets: Images of Greece, Animals, Cats, Flowers, Lesvos, Eresos

To purchase Greek-o-File logos   2 large (9x6cm) for **£2.50** ___
(Notecards & Logos inc UK VAT and P&P)   3 small (6x4cm) for **£1.95** ___

I enclose an article / item for consideration (max 3 x A4 pages, 2,000 words) ___
(Free copy of book supplied to contributors of articles printed of at least 1 page)

Under the terms of the Data Protection Act we do NOT supply names & addresses to
others, but may send mailings about appropriate products from our offices.

Optional Additional Information:

Favourite Greek destination(s) _____ _____
(max 3)

Age Group   Less than 30 ☐   31-45 ☐   46-60 ☐   61+ ☐

Greek-o-File™ Company Reg. 3620858, VAT Reg GB 711 1751 75